Jerk Radar

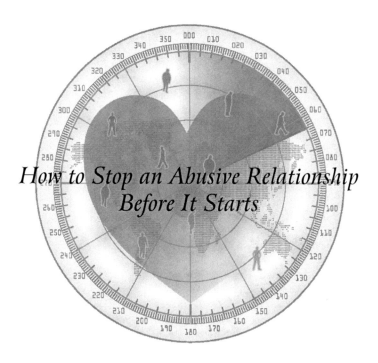

How to Stop an Abusive Relationship
Before It Starts

Stephen T. McCrea, m.s.

INKWATER
PRESS

Portland • Oregon
INKWATERPRESS.COM

Publisher: Inkwater Press | www.inkwaterpress.com

Paperback
ISBN-13 978-1-59299-740-4 | ISBN-10 1-59299-740-6

Kindle
ISBN-13 978-1-59299-741-1 | ISBN-10 1-59299-741-4

Printed in the U.S.A.
All paper is acid free and meets all ANSI standards for archival quality paper.

1 3 5 7 9 10 8 6 4 2

This book is dedicated to the many contributors to The Board, past and present, whose courage and wisdom have inspired this book.

It is also dedicated to the millions of domestic abuse survivors, those who have left, those who are leaving, and those who remain. May this book help you take the next step on your path to a joyful life!

TABLE OF CONTENTS

Acknowledgments

No book can be created without the help and support of a team. I have had plenty of support over the almost four years it took me to write and publish this work, and I would like to take a moment to thank those who helped me along the way.

First, I'd like to thank the incredible supporters on The Board, whose wisdom planted the seed that eventually grew into *Jerk Radar*. Most of all, I'd like to thank TK for her many contributions, both in terms of stories and emotional support, both for the book and in other areas of my life. I'd also like to thank KK, BC, AS, KC, SG, C, CF, JS, AH, CB, SM, TR, JD, SK, L, AG, CH, BK, SA, MT, FS, EG, IM, Anonymous, and Anonymous from Germany, from Indiana, from Australia, from Vermont, and from the UK as well as anyone whose stories did not appear, for sharing their stories and allowing me to publish them. You have told the story in a way I could not have done on my own. I know that your courage in sharing will help others learn from your experiences.

I also want to acknowledge KE, J, and L for creating the wonderful website and online support community that has helped so many survivors get away and stay away over the years, and for welcoming me to become a part of that community.

Extra special thanks go to "Jan" and to "Annie" for allowing me to interview you and share your stories with the readers, as well as for your logistical and emotional support – I love you both!

Thanks to all of my colleagues at work, including my special CASA volunteers, and especially to Trudy and Ruth, for listening to all of my many stories and ideas over the years – your support was far more important than you may imagine.

Thanks also to my wonderful wife, Ginny, and to my three boys, Kevin, Sean, and Patrick, for their reliable support through those many hours at the computer, and for many supportive discussions.

My deep appreciation goes out to Sean, Steve, Linda, Masha, and all the other folks at Inkwater Press for understanding and believing in *Jerk Radar* and helping make this concept a reality.

Thanks to the many authors (Lundy Bancroft, especially) and professionals who have helped enhance and deepen my understanding of what a Jerk is really all about.

And last but not least, my thanks to the many hundreds of abuse survivors who have had the courage to share their stories with me over the years. I have learned more from you than from any book or training course I could have taken, and your spirit is with me on every page I have written. This book is truly for all of you.

If only one of you is helped to escape from or avoid getting involved with a Jerk as a result of this writing, it will have been worth every minute.

STM, February 2012

Introduction

MARK AND JAN MADE AN AWESOME DOUBLES TEAM.[1] THEY'D MET AT the local courts and found they played so well together, they could beat most of the men's teams. They started dating, and Mark turned out to be quite the romantic – he took her to fancy restaurants, treated her to trips to the country, and even took her on an overnight surprise trip to a nearby city, where he wined and dined her before taking her back to a hotel for the night.

Mark wanted things to move along fast. He wanted Jan to move in with him within only a couple months, offering his place as a way for Jan to get away from having to live with her parents. He asked her to be his secretary. He seemed comfortable having them merge their lives together. As they got to know each other better, Jan discovered Mark had a controlling streak. She realized that he might be trouble after an incident where he wouldn't let her out of his sauna when she was feeling sick, and she ended up vomiting on the floor. She also noticed that he'd been saving receipts from all of their romantic dinners. When she asked him about it, she found out he'd been taking them off on his taxes as a business expense.

She soon broke it off and found another doubles partner. It had

---

[1]   Annie, Jan, Mark and Larry are real people, though their names have been changed. These things really happened to them. We'll be following their stories throughout the book, as well as hearing from other survivors of Jerky relationships about how their relationships started out.

been an intense couple of months, but she decided it wasn't worth it. She wished they'd stuck to tennis.

Annie had known Larry since high school. They'd talked sometimes but never went out on a date, and she thought of him as a friend. When they met at a class reunion ten years later, she was surprised to find him pursuing her romantically. While she rebuffed his early advances, he was very persistent, and also seemed remarkably willing to help her with financial issues she was facing. Before long, they were dating and she thought she'd found her life partner.

A year later, she was living 3000 miles away in his home, she was unexpectedly pregnant with his baby, and she found he was being increasingly verbally abusive, destructive of her prized possessions and even overtly violent to her. She felt confused, trapped, and isolated. She ended up calling the police and having him arrested when he tried to choke her and she feared for her life. It took her a couple of years and a move across the country to escape him, and fully recover to a more normal life.

❧

Has anything like this ever happened to you? Have you ever been in a relationship that seemed great to start with, but ended up being a complete disaster? Have you ever wondered why it happened, or how you can keep it from happening again?

It's a hard reality. Much as we might not want to admit it, some people are Jerks.

Some are obvious right from the start: "I'm all about me and I don't care about you at all." Others are more subtle. They seem nice enough, even very charming and generous and kind. But sometime down the road, you realize they are only out for themselves and see you as an object for them to use.

Most of us like to see the good in people. We like to believe that everyone is kind-hearted deep down inside. It goes against our nature to label someone as evil or even just a Jerk. We have learned that we should love everyone, that those who act badly are really just hurting, and that enough love can heal any situation. Sadly, this belief sometimes gets us trapped in situations where we can be taken advantage of.

This book is written for those who have been taken in by a charming person who ended up being a Jerk. Far too often, good-hearted people are fooled by these smooth talkers and end up living a miserable life of abuse, being suddenly abandoned for another woman, suffering an ugly breakup, or painfully freeing themselves from a dangerous relationship. If you have ever had this kind of experience, I'd like to do something to help make sure this doesn't happen to you again. I'd also like to help those who are dating now to avoid ever falling into this kind of trap.

I have worked with many hundreds of abuse survivors over the years. One of the most common questions a survivor asks is: "How could I have predicted this?" Or "Why didn't I see this coming?" Survivors often feel stupid or incompetent when they realize the extent to which they have been deceived. They often question if they might have somehow caused their partner to turn from the lovely person they first met into the inhuman monster they have just escaped. But the truth is, they never met a lovely person. They met a very good con man (or woman) who took them in with their charm and romance and didn't show their true colors until it was too late.

Many other people have not experienced a high level of abuse, but simply notice that they seem to fall for partners like Mark who appear nice at first but turn into self-centered Jerks once they have established a steady relationship. Some have had this experience over and over again, to the point that they conclude one of two things: 1) all men (or women) are Jerks, or 2) for some reason they can't understand, no one nice will ever want to go out with them.

If this sounds like you, then you have chosen the right book to read. The focus of this book is to answer this question: How can you predict when a person will turn out to be a Jerk, even if they seem to be a normal or even incredibly wonderful person at first glance?

You will see that there are signs which can be read early in a relationship that are very good predictors of later abuse or just plain Jerkiness. I will also share some effective ways of testing out your partner for Jerky tendencies without appearing weird or paranoid or putting people off.

You will also hear a lot of stories from people who have survived the worst of abusive situations. Besides Jan and Annie, I collected hundreds of examples of Jerky behavior from Jerk survivors from around the world. These are real people sharing their real personal experiences of what their Jerky partners were like when they first started out. Some got out of the relationship fairly fast, but others spent years trapped in verbally, physically, and/or sexually abusive relationships with the worst kind of Jerks you can imagine. They will share with you what their Jerky partners looked like early in their relationships, and you will quickly see that none of them was obviously mean or abusive at the beginning. They will show you that the seemingly nicest guys can end up being extremely abusive and dangerous.

I do have to warn you, though. This book will not seem very romantic. In fact, you might think I am spoiling any chance of romance you will ever have with my mean-spirited practicality. But sadly, you will see that much of what passes for "romantic" in our culture is actually a potential red flag for abuse. You will see how manipulation, jealousy, aggressive pursuit of an unwilling partner, even stalking behavior, are all regarded as "romantic" in our movies, novels, and sometimes even children's stories. In order to get your Jerk Radar working, you may have learn how to rewire a few of these cultural expectations, at least temporarily, so you can do a thorough screening before allowing yourself to fall head over heels for Mr. or Ms. Right.

What is essential in detecting a Jerk early on is being intentional in your relationship decisions. Being swept off your feet sounds great in romantic films, but in the real world, it usually means you wake up with a big lump on the back of your head wondering what it was that hit you. This book will help you keep your feet in the most intense romantic whirlwind, so you can take a moment to figure out whether this new beau is really a dream come true or a nightmare about to begin!

IMPORTANT NOTE

The techniques and strategies in this book are designed to detect Jerkiness and abusive tendencies *early on* in a relationship. If you are already in an abusive relationship, some of the things I suggest can be extremely dangerous! You can certainly use this book to go back to the beginnings of your relationship and see if your current partner initially displayed Jerk signs you may have missed. But an abusive person who feels possessive of you may feel very threatened if you start asserting yourself in the ways I suggest in this book.

A very simple test is to imagine what s/he would do or say if you asked some of the challenging questions in this book. If you're worried s/he might become aggressive or violent, don't bother with the quiz – instead, call for help right away!

If you feel you are in a relationship where you are scared or intimidated by your partner, or feel in any way confused, blamed, trapped or unable to get away, please call your local domestic abuse hotline and get some support.

In the USA, call 1-800-799-SAFE or go to www.thehotline.org.

In Canada, call 1-800-363-9010.

In the UK, call Women's Aid at 0808 2000 247.

In Australia, call 1800 200 526.

For other numbers, visit www.hotpeachpages.net for a listing of shelters and abuse programs worldwide.

CHAPTER 1

What Is a Jerk?

FOR THE PURPOSES OF THIS BOOK, A JERK IS DEFINED AS A PERSON WHO puts his/her own best interests above anyone else's. This is not to say that anyone who looks out for him/herself is a Jerk. To the contrary! Learning to look out for yourself is the number one antidote to Jerkiness. I want everyone reading this book to be very clear that it's OK to take care of yourself and protect yourself from potential harm. In fact, it's essential to your survival.

But Jerks are people who are *only* motivated by their own interests. They may be very aware of other people's needs, and in fact, be able to meet the needs of others artfully and with seeming sincerity. The problem is *not* that they lack the ability to understand the needs of others. It is that they choose to meet the needs of others only when it has some benefit to them. To Jerks, you are a means to an end, and that end is making themselves feel better, regardless of the effect on you.

"All About Me"

Jerks are people who just don't care. They don't care if they hurt your feelings, they don't care if they use you, they don't care if they betray your trust, they don't care if they leave your life in a smoking wreck, as long as THEY get what THEY want. A Jerk is "all about me" all the time.

Jerks come in all shapes, sizes, races, genders, styles, religions, political persuasions, and sexual orientations. They may be bankers, janitors, housewives, CEOs, social workers, teachers, bus drivers, or any other profession you can name. They can be homeless wanderers or own a million-dollar mansion. They can be teenagers, middle aged, or seniors in a nursing home. What they have in common is a willingness to hurt or harm other people or organizations in order to meet their own needs.

For example, Annie's partner, Larry, was an intelligent, hard-working man who always had a good job. He owned his own house in a nice neighborhood and was active in the community. He even volunteered to deliver "meals on wheels" for the elderly in his free time. And Mark, Jan's partner, was an HVAC salesman with a college education and a nice apartment in the suburbs, who hung out at the local tennis courts. Neither of them appeared on the surface to be mean, controlling or violent, and most of their friends and associates would have considered them nice guys. But in the end, their selfishness became clear, despite how they appeared on the surface.

Two Kinds of Jerks

Now, as I said in the Introduction, there are some Jerks who are obvious. Everyone knows they are Jerks – they are, in fact, proud of being Jerky and will let you know that being self-centered is just the smart way to be. I have never minded these people all that much. They are being clear about where they are coming from, and if you want to be with them, you know what you are getting into. As long as they don't need something from you personally, it's pretty easy to stay clear of them. Of course, if they are your boss or your school teacher or someone with some control over you, it can still be awful to be around them, but at least you know what they are up to and can take measures to defend yourself or escape from their influence.

But there is a whole other breed of Jerks, who are in my view much more common but a lot harder to detect. These Jerks are the smooth talkers of the world, the charmers, the ones who could sell you the Brooklyn Bridge and leave you feeling like you got a great deal. We've all seen these people around and heard stories of them, usually in the context of fraud – identity thieves, con men, snake oil salesmen. They tell a good story and are excellent actors, and people seldom can tell what they're about until it is too late.

It is bad enough running into these folks on the street or in a store or shop. In those cases, it's usually money that is at stake, and while losing money is a bad thing, one can always get more money. It is a whole other story when the thing they are selling you on is a relationship.

Why the Jerk Gets the Girls

I remember being in high school and noticing what I considered a very baffling phenomenon. There were a certain number of guys who were highly popular with the girls and who could generally go out with almost anyone they wanted. The girls fell all over themselves trying to get a date with these popular dudes, but I thought that anyone looking at their behavior could easily see that they were self-centered, egotistical Jerks who used and disposed of girls the way most people throw away used tissue paper.

And yet, somehow, they were the most popular boys. Why?

Because they knew how to work people. They understood how to make you feel like you were missing out if you weren't with them, and they used this skill in a ruthlessly self-centered way. They could lie and swear on a stack of Bibles they were telling the truth. They could go out with two girls at once and get the girls to blame each other rather than understanding that the boy was the cause of both of their suffering. They could get people to do things they would never otherwise do, just to be thought cool.

For a really good example of this, I highly recommend the movie, *John Tucker Must Die*. John is the classic manipulative Jerk who is going out with three girls at once but keeping it secret, supposedly because his parents won't let him date. Besides being a very funny movie, watching his behavior can give you some insight into how this kind of Jerk really operates.

Maybe the reason I could see this so clearly is that I had no investment in being cool. I had long since given up on being in the "in" crowd, so I was always an observer rather than a participant in these social dramas. And the more I watched, the more I was forced to conclude that these Jerks had a certain amazing skill that enabled them to fool others into thinking they were sincere, caring, and very important people with whom anyone would be fortunate to be friends. I sometimes envied them that skill. But it was even more amazing to me that they could live with themselves after all the damage they did to the people who thought of them as friends or lovers.

So I started to wonder: how did they do it? And how was it that I could see them as Jerks and others seemed to worship the ground they walked on?

It was only many years later that I started to connect the dots between these people and domestic abuse. Over time, after I had worked with many survivors of abuse and seen and heard about these Jerks in action, a picture started to emerge of how these socially skilled individuals were able to use common cultural expectations and fears to manipulate other people into seeing them as something they were not.

Which eventually led to the concept of "Jerk Radar." I figured that if I could share some of these observations with readers, that you could then start to see these people for who they are earlier in the process and possibly escape their clutches unharmed.

I don't want to suggest that there are two distinct groups of partners, Jerks and non-Jerks. There is clearly a spectrum of Jerky behavior, and some people will fall into an intermediate zone of "kind of Jerky – not sure if I want to put up with this or not." But there is a certain boundary beyond which a partner's selfishness will exceed any reasonable person's tolerance. This book will help you find where that boundary is for you, and help you to detect your potential partner's true level of selfishness while he is still pretending that he cares about you.

How This Book Can Help

The rest of this book is dedicated to the two important aspects of escaping the control of a Jerk. The first is a short introduction to the cultural assumptions and expectations Jerks tend to use to make their game work. The second is devoted to looking at the actual tactics Jerks often use, and suggesting some specific tests for detecting low-level Jerkiness at the earliest opportunity. Between the two, I hope you will develop a new and more thorough ability to screen out Jerks from your list of potential friends and lovers. We will end with the Jerk Radar Quiz, designed to give you a semi-mathematical way to determine just how Jerky your partner looks from a big-picture perspective.

Some of what I say in this book may seem odd, or maybe even uncomfortable. I may be asking you to question some very basic assumptions you may have about men, women, romance, and relationships. I ask you to be patient at those moments of discomfort, and remember that the purpose of the book is to help you see through how you are being manipulated into seeing Jerks as desirable people. This won't happen without taking a hard look at some of those assumptions, and that can be challenging for anyone.

I ask you to take a moment and check in with yourself if something I'm saying gets an emotional reaction from you. Is the reaction because what I'm saying isn't true? Or is it because it means you may have to re-think some things you've always taken for granted? Without going through some soul-searching, all the tests in the world will be of no use to you, because you won't want to accept the results. So hang in there and keep reading until you get the whole picture, and check in with yourself to see which of the social myths and beliefs I refer to may be leaving you vulnerable to a Jerk Attack. The ones you react to the strongest may be the very ones you have to work hardest to change if you want your Jerk Radar to be in full working order.

I must apologize for one thing in advance. I will be referring to Jerks as "he" and their victims as "she" throughout the book. This is not because all Jerks are men – there are plenty of female Jerks, as well as male victims and same-sex Jerky relationships. However, the vast majority of my experience and observation is with women who were victimized by men, as are most of the examples from the survivors I have spoken with (though I do have one male contributor). There will no doubt be a lot of behavior that I talk about which would apply to female Jerks, or to male victims, but because of differing cultural expectations, female Jerkiness takes on some different forms that I have not studied extensively. So for this book, I will have to confine myself to the male Jerk in relationship to a female partner, as that is what I know the most about.

It is also true that most of my observations have been with western European populations, and the stories, myths and assumptions in other cultures will no doubt lead to some different Jerky strategies in other cultures, which I haven't been able to observe as closely, though I am sure many of the basics (such as irresponsibility and lying) will be observed across all cultures.

I hope with time and experience to be able to expand on the range of cultural and gender situations covered in the book. Meanwhile, I would encourage others interested in this area to research and write about these other aspects of Jerk-ology. I'd love to know what you discover.

CHAPTER 2

Cultural Training

BEFORE WE GET STARTED ON THE PRACTICAL SKILLS OF DETECTING JERKS early on, we need to make sure that our eyes are completely open. It is important to know what you personally are looking for in a relationship, and what vulnerabilities you may have that a Jerk can exploit. It is also essential to understand how Jerks use our cultural expectations to blind us to their unstated intentions. Otherwise, your Jerk Radar will be flashing loud and clear and you will end up ignoring it, because you won't want to believe what you are seeing.

Most of us don't really operate in a thoughtful or intentional way when it comes to relationships – we are more likely to be emotional and impulsive about our relationship choices. Most of us are looking for a romantic relationship to meet a lot of our needs for companionship, intimacy, sexual satisfaction, and long-term stability. We tend to get very excited about a potential relationship and make a lot of decisions based on how we feel at the moment. We tend to put on our "rose-colored glasses" and look for the good in our new partner and dream of the perfect relationship developing. While this kind of attitude is very understandable, it unfortunately makes us vulnerable to the predatory Jerks we have been talking about.

The kind of "smooth operators" I am referring to in these pages will be experts in using cultural assumptions to manipulate you into believing that they really care about you, love you deeply, and are dedicated to your welfare. They will make it seem as if they want to meet all of the needs we mentioned above, while their real motivation is to create confusion and mystery so as to get you under their control. And they do this largely by taking advantage of common cultural myths and beliefs about male-female relationships and using these to blind you to their true intentions.

Examining Common Assumptions

I want to start us off by making some observations about certain cultural beliefs and myths about relationships that we are taught to believe in as children. This learning comes to us from many sources: fairy tales, books, TV shows, advertisements, movies, family, friends, and by observing those around us.

These assumptions are often so generally accepted that we are often not even aware that they exist – they are just things that "everybody knows" to be true, like snow falling in January and people driving on the right side of the road. It is only when we step outside of our usual surroundings that these assumptions ever come to light. For instance, if you go to Australia, you find that January is mid-summer and people drive on the left. You may have known these things to be true intellectually, but it still seems really odd when you are actually driving through a January heat wave on the freeway in the far left-hand lane!

So I am going to ask you to step outside of your usual assumptions for a short while and take a look at some things about relationships you may believe to be true. I am not saying these things are wrong to believe – I am just going to identify them as beliefs rather than facts, and show how abusive people can sometimes use these beliefs to fool you. And I'm going to give a glimpse as to how you may have learned these beliefs, so you can at least have a chance to step back for a moment and have the opportunity to believe something different about a Jerky person when he tries his moves on you.

This is one of those areas where you may find yourself feeling uncomfortable with what I'm suggesting. I'm really not trying to ruin your ability to enjoy romantic movies or children's fairy tales. But it is very important to be more explicit about what you believe a relationship is all about if you are to be rigorous in screening out Jerks. Operating on the myths below will leave you vulnerable in ways you aren't even aware of. So I apologize for any disillusionment I may cause, but I promise you, it will be worth it by the time you get to the end of the book.

There have been whole books written on this topic in great depth, and university courses are taught on the subject. I don't claim to be an expert in this area. I encourage anyone interested to read more about it, because it's a fascinating topic in itself. But for our purposes, I'm only sharing what little I've discovered that applies directly to the question at hand: how do these Jerks do their dirty work, and how can you keep yourself from falling for it?

Fairy Tales

Let's start with fairy tales. These are the stories of our early childhood. In the USA, we're talking about things like "Sleeping Beauty," "Snow White," "The Frog Prince," and "Cinderella." These are stories that most every child who grew up here has heard or read, and many of them have been made into movies or plays or TV shows as well. There may be others in your country or culture that I'm not aware of, but stories of this type will exist regardless of where you come from or how you were raised.

These stories are often referred to in conversations, and when they are, everybody is assumed to know what is meant. For instance, when someone refers to "the Big Bad Wolf," almost everyone knows immediately that this refers to the wolf in the "Three Little Pigs." The Disney tune, "Who's Afraid of the Big Bad Wolf?" can be sung and recognized instantly by almost anyone of my generation who grew up in the USA.

These stories seem charming and harmless, interesting stories that amuse children at bedtime or allow you to pop on a video to keep your kids engaged while you pay the bills or cook dinner. But they are actually full of very interesting messages about what boys and girls and men and women are supposed to do in relationship to each other. And some of those messages play right into the hands of a skilled Jerk.

For instance, how many fairy tales involve a girl/woman being rescued or lifted above her station by a prince or other man of power? It's a total cliché in our culture – we all refer to it as the myth of living "happily ever after." But what does this say about male-female relations? Men are powerful and rescue women from bad situations. Women are not powerful and need men to rescue them. And once you are rescued by the "right man," you will live happily for the rest of your life.

Now, how does this relate to Jerk detection? It's quite simple: a clever Jerk will *pose* as the "Knight in Shining Armor" (another common cliché.) He will assume the role of "rescuing you" from some situation, be it a rough upbringing, poverty, a prior abusive relationship, or a bad job, and will assure you that you will "live happily ever after" if you just stay with him. He'll put you on a pedestal, "treat you like a Princess" (yet another cliché) and make your life seem wonderful, just because he is there.

This is straight out of the fairy tale! He is "the one" you've been waiting for, and if you are a female in a Western culture, you have almost certainly been trained to believe in this kind of "rescuing." So you end up believing in him and letting him "rescue" you. Once this happens, he's got you believing in the fairy tale. He can now take things a long way before you start to suspect that he was less than honest with you when he promised you that wonderful life.

I want to stress here that there is nothing wrong with having a man come into your life and help you make your life better. I do believe in love and relationships and genuine helping energy. And almost all men are similarly trained to act the rescuer role, and most often are genuine in offering their help. So I don't want you to be suspicious of anybody who pulls over to help you change your tire or wants to hear about your crappy family upbringing.

What I do want is for you to be aware that *you* may be looking for this kind of "knight," and an abusive person may well see this about you and use that need to his advantage. I want you to ask yourself a couple of hard questions: am I looking for a man to make my life OK – to live "happily ever after" with? And: has a man ever used this need to fool me into thinking he was something that he was not?

If you answered "yes" to either of the above questions, you are absolutely not alone in doing so. It is the most common way a Jerk hooks in a victim. Being aware of this kind of vulnerability is an absolute necessity for good Jerk screening, because these unknown assumptions are the tools of the Jerk's trade. Once you know what they are, you will be better able to see a Jerk using them to distract you from his true intentions.

What follows are some other common themes from fairy tales and other cultural media which you will want to be aware of. Take a moment and see how strongly our culture reinforces these ideas, and how strongly you may hold them.

Relationship Myths

Myth #1: The beautiful woman gets the man

This is possibly the most common and thoroughly-believed myth that our culture puts forward. Everywhere you look, you see evidence to support this assumption. TV and movie actresses have to be beautiful, while fat and ugly male actors are able to succeed. Female models for clothing, cosmetics, and magazine covers have unnaturally clear skin, bodies that set an unattainable standard, perfectly manicured fingers and gorgeously sculpted hair. The message is clear:

the pretty girl gets the man. But perhaps you will be surprised to learn that we first learn this message in common fairy tales.

Consider the message in "Snow White": The evil queen has a magic mirror that shows her to be "the fairest of them all." But one day, Snow White surpasses her in beauty and therefore has to be killed. Here we see beauty portrayed as a competition, and only the "fairest of them all" can win.

Eventually, Snow White is poisoned and verging on death. But the Prince comes by and sees how beautiful she is, and therefore kisses her and brings her back to life. One can only wonder what would have happened if she were ugly? Would the Prince have kept on riding and left her in a coma? It is not compassion for her situation, but her beauty which moves him to intervene. Of course, she lives "happily ever after," but only because she was pretty enough to attract the Prince who saves her from her fate. She is, in effect, rescued by her beauty.

Other fairy tales have this same theme: "Sleeping Beauty" (the Prince broke into the castle because he'd heard rumors of her beauty), "Cinderella" (the Prince came to find her again because he was struck by her beauty), and "Beauty and the Beast" (the Beast holds her hostage because he "loves her" for her beauty, as the title and her name suggests). There are many more. I don't mean to criticize these stories as stories – they can be charming and entertaining. I often enjoy them as much as anyone. But I want you to become aware of the message you are being given about the importance of beauty as a survival tool for a woman.

Building on this theme, almost any romantic film you can name sets a beautiful female character in the path of a handsome but often misguided man, and her beauty often plays a key role in convincing him that he should take an interest in her, or even inspires him to reconsider how he lives his life. For instance, it's very common in high school romance movies that a geeky or ugly girl gets a makeover and becomes suddenly popular because now she is beautiful. In the 1999 movie, *She's All That*, a clumsy, glasses-wearing "art geek" (Laney) is courted by a jock (Zack) after he bets his Jerky friends that he can get her elected prom queen. During the process, she is "made over" into a beautiful young lady, and he accidentally falls in love with her, and makes her a popular girl in the school as a result of their association. Zack is eventually forced in shame to reveal his original evil intentions, which Laney is appropriately angry at. But of course, she forgives him in the end, and they "live happily ever after." As one might expect, his beautiful and popular former girlfriend (Taylor) becomes jealous of Laney (even though Taylor was the one who dumped Zach) and tries to sabotage her efforts to become prom queen so that she can get Zack back. Once again, obtaining a boyfriend is framed as a competition where the most beautiful woman "wins" the man of her choice, even when that man was extremely creepy and manipulative from the start.

Even if you resist it, you have been taught from early on that beauty is what attracts a man to a woman, and that women compete with women by trying to be the most beautiful. This message has been repeated to you and to all of us thousands of times in thousands of ways. It is a central part of how we've been taught to view male-female relationships.

Do you feel like you have to be beautiful in order to have a man be interested in you? Do you look at your own body or face and wonder if someone could possibly find it attractive? Are you easily swayed by someone complimenting you on your looks? Do you feel like you need to compete with other women for a man's attention using your appearance as your weapon?

I don't mean to criticize you for having these feelings – they are very common, and generally start very early in life based on this kind of story line. But I want you to be aware of this, because any Jerk worth his salt knows that complimenting a woman's appearance is a good way to "soften her up" and make her think he's a good guy.

It's also a pretty common tactic for a Jerk to subtly suggest that he COULD find someone else if you don't do what he wants. This plays on the "beauty as competition" theme that the evil queen introduces in "Snow White." Any time you feel you are competing with other women for a man's attention, you will want to take a step back. Odds are, this man is a Jerk who is using this cultural theme to play you off against each other. Focusing on the competition will keep you from looking to see if this is a person you really want to be around.

At this point, many women raise the argument, "But men ARE most attracted by looks! Whether or not they've been taught to, this is the reality that women face." And there is a great deal of truth to that. But I would revise this to say that SHALLOW men are the ones most concerned with conventional good looks – in fact, in my experience, Jerks are the *most likely* people to use physical appearance as their main criterion for choosing a woman.

I'd say that your physical appearance is your "advertising," and definitely plays a role in whether someone will come up and speak with you. But it doesn't always play out the way you expect. I, for instance, was terrified of "beautiful women" in high school, figuring there was no way they'd be interested in me. There are at least two examples where I sadly discovered years later that this was not at all the case – if I had showed any interest at all, they would have responded, even though I was a total "wallflower." Who knows who might have been interested in me if I'd actually spoken to them?

But I was and am a "nice guy." I really cared about the person I might be going out with, and I also cared about the possibility of being rejected. I was incredibly shy! Someone would have had to make it really clear they were interested in ME before I'd ask them out, no matter how beautiful they were. So all the beauty in the world would not have been sufficient to get me to approach you.

Of course, the Jerks had no such compunctions. They would ask anybody out in a second. They didn't care about being rejected, as they were mostly planning to use the girl anyway, and would generally pick "good looking" girls because it raised their own status as a cool guy. They came across as self-confident and assertive, and they found the best-looking girls and asked them out, and set them up to compete with each other, just like Taylor competed with Laney for Zack. Just like the Queen competed with Snow White for the title "fairest of them all."

I don't mean to play down looking your best as a means to attract male attention. It definitely plays a role, even for a former geek like me. But think carefully about what you are advertising, because you may be attracting just the kind of person you want to avoid.

And once you've made the connection, a whole lot of different factors come into play. I did a few internet searches on "what attracts a man" vs. "what does a man want in a long-term relationship?" Give it a try – you will find that the answers differ greatly. Physical appearance is very important in initial attraction, but appears to play a much more minor role for those looking for commitment. So if you want a man for a long-term relationship, don't spend all your time and energy on looking attractive. At some point, you've got his attention, and it's time to rise above the "happily ever after" myth and see what he's really got to offer.

Myth #2: You can help a "bad boy" become good

This theme is best seen in the fairy tale, "Beauty and the Beast." In this story, Beauty's father is kidnapped by the Beast for trying to take a rose from his garden. Beauty agrees to become the Beast's prisoner in exchange for releasing her father, and is held against her will in a foreign castle. She is treated with decency and given every luxury, but is clearly a captive who is not allowed to leave. The Beast forces her to eat dinner with him every night, asks her nightly if she'll marry him, which she refuses. But he speaks with her daily and she begins to empathize with the Beast, as does the audience. He finally allows her to leave after she becomes very homesick, and only with the promise that she will return in a week. When she fails to keep her word, due to the designs of her jealous sisters, she eventually discovers that the Beast is dying of a broken heart. So she returns and declares her love for him, at which point, he turns into a handsome prince. And they live, not surprisingly, "happily ever after."

Once again, this story can be read for enjoyment – I am not intending to criticize it as a story. What I want to point out is the message that it sends about relationships. The Beast is unreasonably angry about Beauty's father taking a single rose from his garden. He is ill-tempered enough to hold him prisoner for life, or in some versions, to kill him for this simple offense. He essentially does a hostage exchange for his daughter, and Beauty is kind and self-sacrificing enough to agree to suffer so her father can go free. The Beast treats her "kindly" but is holding her prisoner. So far, this guy is looking pretty abusive! But Beauty eventually gets to know the Beast and comes to be friends with him despite his ugliness and despite his ill treatment of her (which is never actually identified as such in the story – she never says, "I can't love a person who would hold my father or me captive over a flower.")

When she leaves, he is devastated, even though he really has little idea who she is (except that she's beautiful). Beauty somehow feels obligated to come back to save him from his suffering, despite the fact that he has wrongfully held her prisoner for months on end. And in the end, realizes that she loves him, which magically transforms him into the handsome prince she's been dreaming about!

A couple of things are very disturbing about this picture. For starters, Beauty has not chosen to associate with this person – he has tricked her father into allowing her to be his captive. Yet somehow, she has developed a sense of obligation to the Beast, to the point that when she fails to return, she feels somehow responsible for his impending death. This theme is repeated in many fairy tales and especially in romantic movies – the man falls in love with the woman, and because he does, she is responsible for his pain if she doesn't return his "love," even if he "makes mistakes." Many modern movies, and in particular, popular love songs build on this theme. Listen to the lyrics on the radio for a half an hour and you'll see what I mean.

Jerky men often use this theme to keep women from leaving when they start to get fed up with the Jerk's behavior or just aren't that interested – "Come on, you know how much I love you! Give me another chance to prove I've changed." The woman is supposed to feel guilty that they are "hurting his feelings" by leaving, no matter how badly he has treated her.

Look at your own experiences and see if you haven't seen this tactic used on you. Has a guy done something harmful and then begged your forgiveness, trying to make you feel guilty? How effective was this tactic? Did you feel guilty about "hurting him" even if you had every reason to want to move on?

Secondly, Beauty falls in love with the Beast despite the fact that he has arbitrarily used power and force to make her stay with him against her will. She is so good hearted that she sees past the ugliness and evil behavior to the "good that lies within his heart." Because she finds it in her heart to care about him despite his evil acts against her, he is magically transformed into a good person. Women are taught in many fairy tales and movies that if they are loving and kind enough, they can "help" a misguided and poorly-behaved man become "better" and "learn their lesson," just as Laney converted Zack into a good person in *She's All That*, as described above.

Jerky men often use this theme to convince their partner that "you can help me become a better man" or "I'm so much better with you around." Later on, when things start to deteriorate, the woman then is made responsible for fixing the relationship or is to blame for it not working the way the Jerk expects. It is tremendously common for a woman to be working hard to get her partner to quit drugs, to get a job, to get him to stop sleeping around, to get him to stop hitting her or the kids, to get him to go to counseling, to get him to get help. And any promise of change from the abuser works on this soft spot: "See, he's changing. I'm helping. I'm doing my job as a woman."

Do you get a strong feeling of worth from helping other people improve their lives? (I certainly do!) Have you ever been taken in by a date or partner who seemed so sad or disturbed, but told you he was "so much better" with you in his life? Are you attracted to "bad boys" whom you then try to help reform or improve? If so, this may be an area you want to be very careful about. Again, this is a common feeling and nothing for you to feel ashamed or inadequate about. It's just something you need to be alert for – if you have a big "helping" button, you need to make sure your partner isn't taking advantage of this so he can manipulate you emotionally.

It would be hard to overstate how powerful this theme is and how readily it is used by Jerky guys to convince women to "give them another chance." Don't fall for it! If you don't like him the way he is, don't work to change him. Change is his job, and if he's not motivated to change, you are far better off looking elsewhere for someone who doesn't have these problems that he is wanting you to fix.

Myth #3: If he pursues you, it means he loves you

This theme is observed in many fairy tales and stories, but is probably best demonstrated by "Sleeping Beauty." In this story, a princess is put to sleep by an evil fairy and is cursed to sleep for 100 years. The only way she wakes up is for a Prince to battle through a hedge of thorns to get to her and awaken her with a kiss. Rapunzel has a similar theme of having to overcome obstacles to prove one's love, and Cinderella does as well (having to find one woman of thousands whose foot fits the shoe she dropped). None of these fairy tales are particularly dangerous in themselves, but they do set the stage for the expectation that men who fight for you are the ones that love you most, as well as that a woman in trouble needs a man to get her out of it.

This becomes a lot more troublesome in modern movies and stories, where the message has been twisted into the idea that pursuing someone who tells you to go away is very romantic. This is what happened to Annie in our second story. Larry was clearly told she wasn't interested, but would not take "no" for an answer. Annie eventually gave in, because he appeared to "care enough" to pursue her despite her lack of interest. The results for Annie were quite disastrous.

This myth is best represented in the cliché picture of the man serenading a woman outside of her window, accompanied by a string quartet or a Mariachi band. This is such a common theme that people laugh when they see it – but think of what it is saying: a woman refuses to go out with a man. He seeks out her place of residence and makes a big scene outside of her home. He forces her to pay attention and puts out a lot of energy to show her that she's so important to him that he won't let go until she decides to accept his declarations of love.

This is actually a form of STALKING. The woman has told the man she's not interested, but he won't take no for an answer. He forces his attentions on her and makes it embarrassing for her to say no. He also adds the guilt trip of spending a lot of money or time creating a big show, so that she seems petty for refusing him. The goal appears to be to get her to give up on her resistance in the face of his "love." In many romantic tales and movies, this tactic is successful in getting the woman to change her mind. And of course, "they live happily ever after."

One of the best examples of abuse being reframed as romance is the 1994 movie, *Only You*, starring Marisa Tomei and Robert Downey, Jr. In this film, Tomei is on the verge of marriage, but hears of the existence of a man named Damon Bradley, the man that a Ouija Board predicted would be her true love when she was a child, and she sets out to Italy in pursuit. Downey's character pretends to be Damon Bradley in order to get Tomei to fall for him. After a very romantic evening, he admits he lied to her, and she is appropriately infuriated and throws him out. However, he continues to pursue her with an offer to help her find the person she's seeking, which she eventually accepts. We find out later that he pays someone else to pretend to be Damon Bradley, who is supposed to become very sexually aggressive so that Downey can "save her" from his attack. Once this more devious plot is uncovered, Tomei again dumps him and decides to go back home. By chance, she meets the real Damon Bradley in the airport, but at the last moment realizes that she is no longer interested, because she is in love with – wait for it – Robert Downey, Jr.! Despite the fact that he has intentionally lied to her twice and concocted a gigantic scam to fool her into wanting him, despite the fact that he continued to pursue her twice after she told him to go away, and despite the fact that's she's already engaged to someone else, she ends up deciding to throw over both her fantasy man and her current fiancé and marry him.

I have to admit, I enjoyed the movie the first time I saw it. But the message is just awful! This man was obsessive, sneaky, and disrespectful from the first moment she saw him. He showed a large number of the "red flags" of abuse that we'll talk about below, yet somehow, she ends up falling in love with him. The message seems to be that he couldn't help himself, because he was SO in love with her, so his bad behavior must be forgiven – it's all for love!

An even more severe example is found in the 1998 movie, *You've Got Mail*, starring Tom Hanks and Meg Ryan. In this one, Hanks is a big bookstore boss who intentionally destroys Ryan's small family bookstore to increase his company's profits. But he unknowingly meets Ryan online and starts a very positive and romantic e-mail correspondence. When they decide to meet, Hanks discovers that she's the woman whose business he's set out to wreck. Rather than admitting that he's the one she's been e-mailing with, he comes as himself and pretends that the e-mail correspondent didn't show up. He gets her to talk about the correspondent as if he were a third party and comments on their relationship.

After he finishes wrecking her business, he finds out where she lives and comes over to her house when she is ill, bringing flowers. He literally sticks his foot in the door when she asks him to leave, and forces his way into her home. Rather than calling the police, she ends up starting a friendship with him, part of which is talking about her ongoing e-mail relationship with the man that Hanks knows to be himself. But he continues to deceive her until the e-mailers agree to meet again, at which point it is revealed that he is the one she's been e-mailing with the whole time.

Now I think a healthy reaction to this revelation might very well be to smack him a good one across the face and to call the police to have him arrested for cyber stalking. But instead, she says weakly, "I hoped it was you." And as the movie ends, they are a couple and she is hired by his company to work in their children's book department.

This is a man who intentionally destroyed her family business, who forced himself into her home, who lied repeatedly to her and pretended he didn't know who she was talking to. This is an abusive man. But in the end, he gets the girl. And gets to be her boss in the bargain.

Sounds just a little like Mark wanting Jan to move in and be his secretary...

Again, I enjoyed this movie the first time I saw it, and didn't notice these negative messages until I'd worked for years with domestic abuse survivors. A lot of others enjoyed it, too – it was the number three hit movie the week it came out. This kind of "romance" sells a lot of movies. It's not something you notice unless you look for it.

But Jerks watch these movies, too, and they hear the message: bring flowers, apologize for being dumb or dishonest or downright evil and blame it on love, keep pursuing her no matter how many times she tells you to go away, and in the end, you'll get your girl.

Women have seen them as well, and without thinking about it, they commonly fall for the idea that stalking is, indeed, romantic.

Has this ever happened to you? Did you end up going out with someone who wouldn't accept "no" for an answer? Did you ever keep seeing someone because you felt impressed that they kept pursuing you, even when you didn't really think it would work? How did it work out in the end?

Watch out for anyone who keeps pursuing you after you say "no." There is nothing romantic about it. It's one of the most dangerous red flags I know of.

Myth #4: Bad men aren't bad, they're just misunderstood

When I was looking over common fairy tales to include in this section, I decided to compare how evil characters are represented based on their gender. In doing this, I noticed something really interesting: there are almost NO evil male characters in European-American fairy tales that are represented as human beings. The Big Bad Wolf, the fox in The Gingerbread Man, the Three Bears, various dragons, even The Beast – evil male characters are almost always portrayed as animals. Those that aren't are generally some distortion of human beings – trolls, giants, Rumpelstiltskin. They aren't just men.

By contrast, there is no shortage of women who represent evil characters – the Queen in "Snow White," the evil stepmother and stepsisters in "Cinderella," the stepmother in "Hansel and Gretel," not to mention the various witches, evil fairies, and the like, who turn poor, powerless men into frogs or beasts or trap damsels in towers and so forth. It appears from fairy tales that the vast majority of evil springs from women.

I ran this by my teenage son, and we wracked our brains to think of an evil male character. We finally came up with two: the Pied Piper (who is not purely evil – he's actually being helpful until the men of the town decide not to pay him and then pipes their children out of town with him), and the King in Rumpelstiltskin.

This King is the only clearly abusive male character we could find. He hears from a miller a boast that his daughter can spin straw into gold. He has her held captive and orders her to spin gold under penalty of death. She, of course, has no idea how to do this, and has to promise Rumpelstiltskin her first-born child so he will save her life. The evil King is so pleased, he orders her to do it again and once more threatens to kill her. When she is successful, he tells her if she does it a third time, he will marry her. And he keeps his word.

Oh, my! The only truly evil male character we can locate in any fairy tale, and the victim ends up MARRIED to the perpetrator! And the poor miller's daughter is supposed to feel somehow LUCKY because she married this Jerky guy who was going to kill her for failing to do something that no one had a right to expect her to do.

What's going on here? Is there no such thing as a man with evil intentions? Male characters that do engage in evil actions, like the Beast, usually only do so because they've been cursed by evil women, and good women are able to save them with their kisses and their love. And even the outright evil King in Rumpelstiltskin still "gets the girl" without any further comment on his Jerky behavior.

Jerks are very adept at using this theme to manipulate women into accepting bad behavior. When confronted about abusive actions, even minor ones, a Jerk may break down in tears and let you know how it's all because his abusive dad acted this way. He's trying really hard to get over it but he's had such a rough life, he just needs someone understanding like you to help him get through. He's not evil, he's just misunderstood.

Many people have a visceral reaction against even calling a Jerk by that name when I talk to them about these concepts. They want to believe that no one is really evil, that deep down, there is a good person who can be reached if only they try hard enough. It seems very hard for most victims to look at their Jerky partners and say, "It's not because he's misunderstood or mistreated. He's just plain mean, and he's trying to harm me!" This may be hard mostly because there are just no stories that tell us to look out for abusive men.

Does using the term evil or even Jerk bother you somehow? Is it hard for you to imagine that a man would approach you with the intention of using you or taking advantage of you? Has this ever happened to you in the past? Was it hard to accept that he was up to no good? Did you blame yourself in any way for what he did? Do you still?

This may be the most important myth of all to overcome if your Jerk Radar is to be in full operation. You will need to enter every relationship with the knowledge that some men ARE ill-intended toward you or women in general, and that it may not be obvious at first. I'm not saying to be paranoid and to assume that all men are out to take advantage of you. I am simply asking you to dismiss the idea that men can't be bad, or that even if they are, your love can "fix" them up. Just because someone has an explanation for their bad behavior doesn't mean they won't repeat it on you. And if you don't like their behavior now, when they're putting their "best foot forward," the odds are it will only get worse, no matter how beautiful or wonderful or loving you may be.

Myth #5: "The One"

There is a more recent adaptation of the idea that "someday my Prince will come." It relates back to several of the myths already covered, including the idea that a man is necessary to save you, and the concept of "happily ever after." This is the idea that there is One Person for each of us, and that our job is to find The One, and if we find The One, then we will be magically happy forever, just like in the fairy tales. Many movies, TV shows, and books, including *Only You* referenced in the last section, build on this idea of The One. Marisa Tomei goes off to Italy seeking Damon Bradley only because it was predicted that he was The One for her. She throws over all of her previous plans and even overlooks some very seriously abusive behavior on The One's part, because after all, they were meant to be together. What's a little deception and stalking to stand in the way of True Love?

Of course, abusive Jerks are very familiar with this theme and use it mercilessly early on in a relationship. He gazes into your eyes, and says, "As soon as I saw you, I knew – I knew you were The One for me!" Ah, so very romantic! Unfortunately, he may have said the same thing to the last three girlfriends he had, or even to someone else in the same bar earlier that evening who was savvy enough to know he was full of crap. As you'll see when you read Chapter 5 on intensity, this framing of instant love may often be the first play in an effort to isolate and control you, or at best, to fool you into doing things he wants you to do, even if those things are against your own interests.

Now I'm not saying that I don't believe that people can fall in love quickly, or that they might not be an excellent match. After all, my mom and dad were engaged after knowing each other for just a few short weeks, and they were (reasonably) happily married for over 50 years. But I don't think it's good policy to believe too quickly that someone is "The One" for you, especially if they seem to be wanting to *convince* you that you are "meant to be together." The ways of the world are mysterious, and it is too hard for us mere mortals to know who is and is not meant for us.

Here is where romance and I part company. Basically, I see ALL relationships as having pros and cons, and what you need is not "destiny," but someone with whom the pros outweigh the cons by a big enough margin that you won't end up hating each other a few years down the line. I've seen a very tiny number of relationships where the partners seem so well matched that it approaches "destiny." But 99.9% of the time, even in the best relationships, your partner will do some things that will drive you nuts, and they'll feel the same about you. The real test of a relationship isn't whether you're "meant for each other," it's how you handle it when you find out that your idealized version of your True Love doesn't quite fit with reality. And it's when this idealized phase starts to fade that the true personality of a Jerk comes to the surface.

The purpose of this book is to stop you long before the relationship gets to that point. In order to do this, the idea of The One has to be set aside for a more rational analysis of what this person has to offer, as well as what the cost will be for you. Not nearly as romantic as the movies, but I can guarantee it will be a lot safer for you.

That's the essential message of this chapter: Don't wait for Prince Charming to come and find you. You decide what you want and go look for it. You will have to let go of romantic myths and fairy tales, at least temporarily, if you want to get your Jerk Radar tuned up and fully functioning. You must start off by recognizing that any Jerk worth his salt knows all of the movie lines that are designed to melt your heart. If you're watching a movie or reading a novel, these lines and themes can be very entertaining and enjoyable. But life is not a movie, and believing these things can really happen can leave you vulnerable to the manipulations of a master Jerk. So be aware of this and other messages you've been taught and watch to see how your partner may be using them on you. Once you've made this shift and are looking more critically at your prospective partner, the techniques in the rest of the book should help you steer clear of any Jerk who makes a move in your direction.

CHAPTER 3

Excessive Charm

MY FIRST DATE, HE BROUGHT FLOWERS, TOOK ME TO DINNER AND TREATED ME like a princess. No matter what I did, it was awesome. He brought me a little present at ever date for the first few months. I thought I had found my prince.

He caused me to feel so wonderful about myself, but more wonderful about him – he became my self esteem, he made me feel so great. He would call me just to tell me he missed me and was thinking about me. He would surprise me with visits and bearing presents for me. He told me that I should be treated like a queen because that is what I deserved. He was the perfect man until we married, only a few short months later. He would introduce me to his friends as the perfect girlfriend and say he doesn't know what he did to deserve me. He would tell his friends and family constantly how wonderful I was, in fact, it was a little embarrasing for me. Flowers, candy, jewelry, my favorite author books, surprise trips, everything in those few months we dated. Yes, he spent a lot of money, but thinking back, how cheaply I sold myself.

I remember the first verbal blow I received. I was crushed and wanted to do anything to make him think of me the way he did before. I just wanted him to think of me again in that same way, to think I was wonderful and to love me.

—BC, Pennsylvania, 20 years in abusive relationship

Most people going through a courtship with a potential partner go out of their way to put their best foot forward. They dress well, are polite, listen attentively, try to have a sense of humor, and work to be as genuinely sensitive as they are able to be. This is very normal in our culture, and probably in any culture. We all want to look our best when finding someone we are considering as a possible partner.

A part of this is gift giving. In Western culture at least, it is considered romantic for a man to give a woman flowers, or to purchase her a small gift as a token of his appreciation. It is also considered appropriate in most circles for the man to buy the woman dinner, pay for a movie or a show, or otherwise treat her to something special.

Additionally, we expect courtship to involve a certain amount of charm – making compliments, appreciating good looks or stylish dress, laughing at each other's jokes, talking about topics we agree about, and so forth. All of these things are to be expected, and none of them would be a bad sign in someone seeking a relationship with you. In fact, a person who didn't do any of these things might be someone you'd wonder about – if this is him at his best, what will he be like when the "honeymoon is over"?

Unfortunately, most Jerks know these rules very well and will use them to their advantage. One of the earliest indicators in your Jerk Radar screen should be what I call "excessive charm." This person may have flawless manners. He may be the total and complete gentleman in every way. He may be sweet and thoughtful and generous, and the entire time may be plotting to take advantage of you.

This is where the first myth we mentioned comes into play. The Jerk knows you want him to be floored by your beauty and charm, to be swept off his feet just like the Prince in "Cinderella," so that he'll take you off to his castle and treat you like a Princess as you deserve. The most suave and effective Jerks will play this card early on, putting you on a pedestal and making you feel like you are so amazing that nothing he can do will be too much to let you know how special you really are, as BC explains above.

This is one of those times I'll be accused of being unromantic, and it's true. I don't deny it can feel wonderful to be wined and dined and bought flowers and gifts and treated like a Princess. And assuming the person is genuine in their courtship, there is no reason not to fully enjoy this lovely period in a relationship. But you need to know that the great feelings you are having may be the first move in the Jerk's strategy to get you under his control.

Over-the-Top Generosity

When I talk about excessive charm, I don't mean just holding the door for you or buying you a corsage or treating you to a show. I am talking about a constant barrage of small or large acts calculated to make you feel like this guy is the most wonderful guy in the world. Your date may plan an entire evening and spend hundreds of dollars getting a limo, buying you a new dress, taking you somewhere you have said you would have loved to go, making your favorite meal, or whatever. But it's over the top. It's in excess of what you would normally expect a guy, even one who really liked you, ever to do.

> [He] gave me a brand new 500 dollar guitar 10 days after we started dating, because it was my birthday. He knew it was one of my dreams-life goals to learn to play guitar.
>
> –Anonymous, Germany

> He treated me like a queen, cooked for me, we took a wonderful vacation to Florida, to see my sister. She thought he was wonderful because he treated me so good. When we returned from Florida, he moved in with me, and everything was great – for six weeks. By then I was head over heels in love and I couldn't understand why the charm wore off and the abuse began.
>
> –Anonymous, 65, Indiana, spent 22 years in abusive relationship

All of this has to be considered in the context of whom you

are dating, of course. A person who has little money but buys an expensive ring on your second date is probably going over the top. If your date normally travels by limousine and has a personal driver, getting a limo may be very normal for him and not a bad sign. But take a look and see if he isn't trying a little too hard to impress you.

If you find yourself really surprised, even kind of shocked, that someone would do so much or spend so much just for you, watch out!

Remember how Mark treated Jan initially? Lots of expensive dinners out, trips, and special nights in a hotel, even when they'd known each other only a few weeks? She didn't see it at the time, but his "charm" was the first indication that he was manipulating her to gain control.

Again, there is nothing wrong with romantic gestures. People do them all the time. And you may also run into a person who just tends to go overboard in this arena, but is otherwise quite appropriate. It's not a make-or-break issue, but it is a "red flag" – a sign that means you want to look further into this person.

Excessive Flattery

Another thing to watch for is excessive flattery. A person who, on a first date or even a second or third, is saying things like, "You are the most beautiful woman I've ever seen!" or "I think about you all the time," or "Your hair is so amazing, I dream about it at night!" may be trying to charm you into submission. Similarly, they may seem to be incredibly impressed with your intelligence, your business savvy, or your courage in escaping from a prior abusive situation. Whatever it is, watch for the "over the top" quality where you are SO impressive, SO beautiful, or SO intelligent that they are just knocked off their feet by it.

Stupid Compliments
You were the most beautiful woman at the party.

You don't have a single wrinkle on your face. (age 52)

My friends asked if you were a friend of my daughter's (she was 18 at the time).

You have a body better than most 25 year olds.

I have never seen abs like that – they're amazing.

You are remarkably intelligent, not like most women who only talk about people, not issues.

He said he was never interested in sex until I came into his life (at age 58). He was incredulous at how good the sex was; he didn't know it could be like that.

                    –TK, 59, Canada, abused 10 years before escaping

I would particularly be cautious when there are sexual overtones to the compliments very early in the dating relationship. This may be a sign that the person's objective may be only to have sex or to possess you sexually. This person may see women in general as providing sexual gratification and be grooming you to play that role in their lives.

Always Agrees with You

An excessive charmer may also spend a lot of time asking you questions about you while sharing little about himself. There is a reason for this. In order to get you into the right mood, the charmer has to find ways to agree with you and your views. It's been shown in sales and management and counseling and many other areas that the best way to get human beings to like you and feel comfortable with you is to agree with them about things they think or do or believe. So a clever Jerk will be asking you questions like, "What kind of music do you like?" When you tell them you love country, they love country, too! If you are into jazz, well oddly enough, they think Miles Davis is awesome. If you say you love Beethoven, then the 9th Symphony becomes the next topic of conversation. It's pretty easy to do this without the other person noticing a thing, because we are all very inclined to believe that others who agree with our tastes or opinions do so because they are intelligent enough to notice our own good taste and well-founded wisdom. It rarely occurs to us that we are being manipulated.

So what you want to watch out for is someone who doesn't express any strong opinions or preferences until you have expressed yours. And once you do express them, this person will almost always agree with you, whether it's politics, religion, music, movies, or dinner preferences. They may be evasive when you ask them about themselves, often being noncommittal or turning the question back on you (unless they already know what you think about the area). They will generally volunteer very little about their own thoughts or beliefs or will put forward the most non-controversial views until they can gauge your reactions. Once they know what you think, they suddenly have strong opinions that just happen by chance to coincide with your own.

It is important to note at this point that not ALL Jerks will court you in this way. Some will act pretty normal, and some will be obvious Jerks right from the get-go. But there are a lot of Jerks who are incredibly skilled at this courtship ritual, and who view it as a game or contest that they can succeed at. You are in such cases more the target or objective of the game rather than a person they are getting to know. Even though they will go through all the appropriate motions and will seem completely sincere, they are on a specific mission and the courtship process is just a means to an end for them.

> Lines I fell for… "You're not like other girls." "You are so fit, you'll never be fat!" (This one always bothered me anyway – like he was dictating.) "You have the hottest belly."
>
> **–Anonymous, 35, Vermont, married 5 years to abusive spouse**

> I met my Ex and the next night he turned up at my door. We lived a 1 1/2 hours drive away from each other and

he turned up every night, after work, for a week. He was charming saying things like I was the most beautiful girl in world. He said he told his best mate, the night he met me, that he was going to marry me. He made me feel like the only woman that ever mattered to him."

—Anonymous, 56, Australia, 13-year marriage to abusive spouse

How to Tell the Difference

So how do you tell the difference between a genuine courtship where someone is trying to look their best and a Jerk's game where someone is trying to put one over on you? How can you check without looking paranoid or coming across as a freak?

Here are some simple tests you can conduct without ruining the flow of conversation. These are questions that the normal person will take in stride, but will set the Jerk's mind spinning as they wonder whether you are onto their game.

1) Ask specific questions about him and his beliefs that you haven't already answered. Some examples:

A) What is his favorite music group?
B) Who did he vote for in the last election and why?
C) Where does he come down on a controversial issue such as gay marriage, immigration, or abortion?
D) What does he like to do when he is alone?
E) How does he see men and women the same and different?

Don't tell him what you think – get him to go out on a limb and state his opinion. If you find that the person is unwilling to answer these questions, or is evasive, or consistently turns the question around to you, that is a sign that you may have a Jerk on your hands.

2) Try disagreeing with him on a point where he has expressed his opinion. If he loves country music, and you don't, tell him that and see how he reacts. If he changes what he just said and now claims he really doesn't like country after all, watch out. He's changing what he believes in order to please you. This usually means one of two things, and sometimes both: either he has no sense of who he is and changes in order to please everyone, or he's an abuser who is working to get you to believe that you and he "have so much in common" you should therefore be together. Either way, you are dealing with someone who is not honest and will probably create difficulties for you down the road.

3) If a gift seems excessive, graciously refuse to accept it. "Oh, that is very sweet of you, but I don't think we know each other well enough for me to accept a gift of that nature." See how he reacts to this. If there is pressure on you to receive the gift anyway, such as talk of how difficult it would be to return it now, or how you shouldn't worry about it because he has lots of money, or how you are so beautiful and wonderful that it is worth every penny, or anything that makes you feel he's not accepting that you don't feel comfortable with the gift, you have more evidence that this person is not respectful of your rights and boundaries, which is the essence of what a Jerk really is.

4) If you are noticing he always plans all the evening's activities, try this: don't go along with his "surprise plans" that he has made for you. Tell him you're not in the mood for dinner at the place he chose, but would rather "eat in" this evening. Watch how he handles the change of plans. Some Jerks will become upset (maybe not visibly) and try to talk you into going along with their plan. This type is unable to allow other people to make decisions and will simply not accept "no" for an answer. This is really a very bad sign, and is probably sufficient in my book for you to look for someone else to spend your time with. Any relationship is founded on mutual trust and negotiation. If a person is unable to allow their partner to have any influence on simple decisions such as where you both eat tonight, their need for control is going to lead to a very difficult relationship down the line.

The other reaction to watch for is someone who has made elaborate plans and then is willing to completely drop them as soon as you say "no." It is normal for a person to be at least somewhat invested in their plans, and to express some disappointment or frustration – "Darn, I was really looking forward to this." Or, "Oh, I thought you loved that restaurant!" But they will not try to pester or arm-wrestle you into submission. They will express their feelings of frustration and then be able to move on. A person who is ALWAYS willing to bend to your wishes and appears to have no feelings or reactions at all is probably playing you.

5) **Make your own plans and invite him along**. If he is a very controlling person, he will probably make some efforts to change your plans. "Oh, but I had a better idea for tonight – I got theater tickets for both of us!" (He may not even buy the tickets until after he convinces you that you can't pass up this opportunity.) Or, "we can go there for a while, but my friend is having a party at 8 and I just HAVE to attend!" Again, this kind of thing could happen in any normal relationship, but you are looking for the excessive pressure or unwillingness to be flexible or adapt to your way of doing things. It's also important to keep in mind that some Jerks will just go along with anything you want as an effort to convince you of their devotion. The essential test is to make your plans without consulting him, and see how he reacts. A normal person may have feelings and reactions they will share, but will be flexible about adapting to your plans at least most of the time.

6) **If you are being barraged by excessive compliments, you can stop and ask some challenging questions**. "Wow, you seem to believe I'm walking on water! Can I really be that perfect? Do I have any flaws that you have noticed?" Or "What do you really look for in a woman, and what bothers you?" Or "What kind of

things would make a relationship unworkable for you?" A person who is in excessive charm mode will often have a hard time coming up with answers to these questions, whereas a person who is being genuine will generally have thought about these things and will share their thoughts with you.

This could lead to a very interesting conversation that reveals a lot about the preferences and priorities of your date. A healthy exchange on these points can help move a good relationship forward. It can also make you aware of what limitations you may be up against. But an unwillingness or inability to share potential relationship barriers is not a good sign.

On the other hand, you may get a litany of what is wrong with women, including prior partners (see Chapter 8 for more on this), or may get some subtle hints that being overweight (as Anonymous from Australia reports above) or hanging around too much with one's mother are unforgivable sins. Listen carefully to what is said and try to maintain some objectivity, asking yourself what his responses say about his personality. Look for signs of anti-woman bias, strong sex-role stereotypes, or beliefs in male dominance. The absence of these doesn't mean it's clear sailing by any means, but expression of this kind of attitude early in a relationship is a sure sign that you will want to look elsewhere for a long-term companion.

7) Share some of his charming efforts with a person whom you regard to be objective. Let them know of anything he did or does that has that "over the top" feeling or makes you feel uncomfortable. Ask them if it seems excessive to them or not. Check with several people if you are unsure of yourself. If there is a consistent message that this seems weird or excessive, or even if there is a variety of opinions about it, keep your eyes open.

It is very hard to keep perspective when you are feeling attracted or are getting involved with a new partner. There is nothing wrong with checking your perceptions with others. This is particularly

true if you are feeling head-over-heels "in love" with someone. None of us is rational when we're in that intense, lovely, terrifying roller-coaster feeling of being in love. So why not share with someone a little more objective if there are things that we're not quite sure about? Choose people who you know are honest and don't have a lot of their own issues with men or relationships, and see what they say. It can't hurt, and it might save you from making a big mistake you will live to deeply regret.

CHAPTER 4

Big Ego

A SECOND EARLY SIGN OF A JERK THAT IS SOMEWHAT DIFFICULT TO HIDE is having a large ego. Now I know what you may say: a lot of guys have large egos, and you are absolutely right about that. So this is kind of a "soft" category where many men will score some negative points. As in any of these categories, just having a big ego in and of itself doesn't mean you've got a Jerk on your hands. But it's a warning sign, and if it is combined with other warning signs, awareness of a big ego may help you to stop a bad relationship before anything bad really happens.

So what are the signs of a big ego? Most of us know them well: self-centered in conversation, boasts a lot about accomplishments, competes for attention, jealous of others' attention or success – you are familiar with these obvious signs. But let's take a look at how this plays out early in a dating relationship.

Dressing (Him or You) to Impress

One sure sign of a big ego is an emphasis on "looking good," usually (but not always) in a way that is accepted by others. Abusers are usually conformists on some level, because they are acting a part that they need to act in order to accomplish their goal of controlling the situation. So you will often see them dress up impressively, maybe even a bit "over the top" as we talked about in Chapter 3. Again you have to consider where they come from as you evaluate

this point – a person from a street background may not ever consider dressing up in a coat and tie, whereas a guy from a "high class" family may consider a tuxedo a requirement for taking you to the opera. But every culture has its standards, and within those standards, the average Jerk will try to dress impressively. Even someone who is in rebellion against society, such as a teenager in gangster clothing, will still comply with the expected "uniform" of such a person – the right colors, pants worn sagging, proper amounts of "bling," the right brand of shoes, and so on. The point is, this person will generally dress to impress.

> First thing I noticed was how he would brag about his clothes. He would only buy expensive designer clothes, even when he was broke. And sometimes I wasn't sure if he lied about his clothes – he would say he got his leather boots from Pamplona in Spain, made out of the skin of bulls from the bullfights there; his suit was a designer suit and cost hundreds of dollars.
>
> **–Anonymous, 24, Germany, abused 8 months**

Again, I want to remind everyone that lots of people like to dress up to go out. This alone means very little. But combine this with some of the other "big ego" indicators, and you may have cause for concern. Combine a big ego with a few more indications from other categories, and you can be pretty sure that you have a true Jerk on your hands.

Interestingly, an even more telling question than how your partner dresses is how they expect you to dress. A person who is truly self-centered will see his date as an extension of himself. Hence, if he is to look good, YOU have to look good, and looking good will be defined in his terms. He may also boast to his friends about how pretty you are or how well-dressed you are, as if it is somehow a reflection on his good taste that he chose an attractive woman who knows how to dress well. So if you find early in your relationship that your partner is criticizing your clothing, giving

you lots of "advice" on how to look your best, or purchasing you things that he then expects you to wear, I would be very suspicious. You should have the right to look however you want to. He can tell you how he feels, but when he starts telling you how to dress, you should really take a very hard look at what his real motivations are.

> He was not a sharp, fancy dresser, but was always concerned with appearance. Lots of self-preening in bathroom. And, he was concerned about my appearance. He once said, "You wear sexy underwear, but you could really wear nicer clothes. I'll take you up to (the city) sometime to go shopping." I remember being half-flattered (excited for clothes?) and totally insulted at same time.
>
> —Anonymous, 35, Vermont, 5-year abusive marriage

> When we first met and before we married he was very keen to show me off to his friends and then said, after I'd met them, that they'd all liked me and it was as though it was a feather in his cap. If we were going out to meet friends he would pass comments on what I was wearing and would often say that I should wear something else, as though I was like a possession, a doll, that he could dress up in what he pleased. He told me very frequently, and this was consistent throughout our 25 year relationship, how he showed off about me to people, but I felt very much from the word go that I had certain expectations to live up to.
>
> TR, 25-year abusive relationship

Controlling What You Say

Similar to dress, a Jerky partner may also be very concerned about what you say in public. They may handle this by always making sure that the two of you are alone together, or by making sure that he is in a position to dominate the conversation if you are there.

But if you find yourself being cut short or criticized about what you are saying, if you find yourself being boxed into having to have certain beliefs or express yourself in a certain way, if you are told that you talk too much, or your communication is otherwise being screened for "correctness," you should be concerned. You should not have to screen what you say to make sure it doesn't embarrass him or make him "look bad." Only a very egotistical person would think to control you in that way.

Boasting

Boasting or bragging is another thing we associate with a big ego. Many Jerks (though not all) love to hear themselves talk, and mostly talk about themselves. This may not be apparent at all in your one-on-one communication (which is one reason that Jerks often like to keep you isolated from your friends or his), but in a group setting, it becomes much more obvious. If you find that your date kind of forgets about you around a bunch of his friends and ends up spending a lot of his time telling stories that sound a little questionable or reminding everyone of who he knows or what he's done, you know you've got an ego to manage. As I stated before, this alone is not a deal breaker. But it should be a warning sign that you want to keep your eyes open. Self-centered people seldom make great partners.

> ...he was very concerned about his accomplishments – his job, how much he earned, what he could do – his skills and his goals. His accomplishments were of course always more important than mine. Everything centered around this. If he did anything at all, he'd expect me to tell him how great he is and be thankful and in all awe. If I did something, it was "only natural" and not a big deal.
>
> **–KK, Estonia, 30, 7-year abusive relationship**

Name-Dropping

Another aspect of boasting is name-dropping. A person who wants you to know that they are connected with "big people" is trying to impress you. Especially if some of the connections sound a little questionable, or you know for sure they are made up, you may be in the presence of an egomaniac who is more concerned with how he looks than how you or anyone else feels, or even what is actually true.

> He claims to have descended from Jesus, that yes, he could trace his family tree back to Jesus, and there is something about the south of France and 1066...
>
> –TK, 59, Canada, abused 10 years before escaping

Being a Poor Sport

Big-ego types also have a tendency to be poor sports. They play to win and have a very hard time losing. Games become very serious, and a lot of aggressive "joking" will be noted. This is also a time when attitudes toward women become more pronounced. If you play softball or tennis doubles or basketball with an egotistical guy, prepare for either a lot of criticism of your play, or for him to step in front of you and make the play himself rather than risk letting you "mess up." It is also very interesting to see how a man reacts when his date or partner beats him at something. Most Jerky guys will have a very hard time with this – they will hate to have you beat them at anything, unless they "let you win" to make an impression.

> My husband is very competitive when it comes to sports. He has always thought he was the biggest, the best and everything he does. He is a pitcher for one of the county's slow pitch leagues. He thinks that every time there is a tourney that everybody wants him to be on their team, he thinks that people actually call each other and fight about who gets him to pitch.... If his team loses, he is

in a miserable mood for days, sometimes weeks. Silent, moody etc. I have seen him throw his ball gear across the field.

—Anonymous abuse survivor

You get the idea that basically, whatever he lost at wasn't his fault. And conversely, if I won, it would be because I was lucky at whatever it was and nothing to do with skill. If we played cards with the children I often caught my husband looking at their cards (I was wise to his tricks so was careful not to let mine be seen), so [he was] cheating.... This was a man who would go to any lengths to win by whatever means were possible.

—TR, 25-year abusive relationship

And by the way, a man "letting you win" a lot is not necessarily a good sign, either. It could mean he is either patronizing towards women because he considers them beneath him, or that he's afraid to take you on directly because you might actually beat him. It's a soft sign, but also one to watch for.

You can see signs of this even in everyday conversations, especially when he's talking to someone besides you. A normal disagreement about a sports team or political contest or even a movie or music group can become a contest of wills and logic to see who comes out on top. A lot of women come to expect this from men and consider it par for the course, but I would take note of this tendency and see how frequently it occurs, and how aware your date is of it. It could be just a "fun" activity that he enjoys, in which case he'll be able to laugh about it and back away if he's getting too serious. But the true Jerk will have a hard time admitting he is wrong about anything. This is probably the best ego test of all – the willingness to admit to sometimes being wrong. A person who can't admit he is wrong cannot adapt to a new situation and can't learn from his mistakes. Such a person can make a very dangerous partner.

Reckless Driving

Another one I learned from the survivors who helped me with their stories is that road rage and reckless driving are very common amongst Jerky partners. This makes a lot of sense from the big ego standpoint, as this kind of attitude reflects a belief that "people need to get out of my way," or that he is more important than the other drivers he's endangering, and more important than you as a passenger, for that matter. It can also be an early way of intimidating you – since "road rage" is so common and accepted socially, it can be his way of testing out to see how much you'll tolerate before complaining about his driving or his angry behavior. In any case, driving in traffic is a place where many people tend to let their deeper emotions come to the surface. While a lot of folks get frustrated in traffic, you should not explain this one away, but regard it as an important red flag, especially if it combines with other "big ego" indications. If he can be verbally abusive to other drivers, or even endanger them or you when he's mad enough, there is a good chance you will find yourself on the receiving end of similar abuse one day in the not-too-distant future.

> I dreaded being driven by my ex, so angry did he get with fellow motorists and he took such unnecessary risks. It seemed that nobody was allowed to hold him up and it was a nightmare if we became stuck in traffic.... He always drove very, very close to the car in front and honestly – I almost needed Valium when I got into the car with him. He would also overtake whenever he could, often regardless of safety, because there couldn't possibly be another car on the road in front of him – he had to be in the lead at all times.
>
> –TR, 25-year abusive relationship

> My ex would drive very fast and scary at times, and wouldn't slow down even (especially) when I asked him

to do so since I felt scared. He enjoyed having this power over me and he enjoyed seeing me scared and putting me at risk.

–Anonymous, Germany

SCREENING FOR A BIG EGO

So how do you screen for a big ego (beyond the normal range of male chest thumping)?

Here are some ideas:

1) Check for excessive concern about appearance, especially your own. Dress down a bit for an outing that you are doing together and see how he reacts. Is he surprised? Does he ask you about it at all? Does he suggest that you dress up more? Does he make any critical comments about your dress, either subtly or directly? It's not a problem if your partner notices and comments on your change of style. But if they are upset by it in some way, it may be an indication that you are somewhat of an ornament to this person, and he wants you to look good so he looks good. Comments like, "Hmm, I'm not sure how that will go over at the club," or "I really like shorter skirts – do you have something like you wore the last time?" might seem innocent, but why is this person so concerned about how you look? Is he genuinely worried that you might be uncomfortable? Or is he more concerned you are going to reflect badly on him by your "lack of taste"? If his comments reflect that you have to look "nice" in ways that he dictates, this is a potential sign of trouble.

2) Suggest an activity that requires some risk of not looking his best – try hiking or gardening or painting a room or something that he isn't used to that requires him to get his hands dirty. See how he handles it. Can he roll up his sleeves and do

some work without having to look pretty? Are there activities or jobs that this person considers "beneath him?" These are some soft signs of a big ego. Or try something he might consider "hokey" or "square" like a square dance or going to the zoo or something that puts him outside his comfort zone. Everyone has things they don't like to do, but a person who will never do anything they can't look good at is probably a person whose ego is a bit oversized.

3) Do a little fact checking on any name dropping he may have done. Ask him how he knows so and so, where they work, what kind of person they are, etc. Just act interested and ask questions and see if he gets flustered. If he gets irritated with you for asking or starts making up more and more far-fetched stories, he's making this stuff up to be noticed.

4) Play him in a game where you know you are capable of beating him and see how he does with it. Can he handle losing? Does he let you win? Can he handle friendly competition from a partner, or does he make snide remarks or get overly aggressive?

5) Better yet, watch him play a game "with the boys." Something that will bring out the most competitive side in him. See how he handles losing, bad calls by the referee, or someone else getting the spotlight. You can get a similar hint by watching him watch a sporting or other contest he cares about. Does he get down on the refs a lot? Does he denigrate the other team or the city or country they come from? Does he get visibly upset at his own team for failing him (other than momentary frustration over a botched play)? Does he take it just a little too seriously?

6) Challenge him to learn something new that he'll have to be a beginner at. See if he can fail with good humor. See if he's even willing to try something that may embarrass him. Most real egotists have a hard time doing something they're not already good at and tend to avoid it like the plague. A more normal person

would have fun trying something new and would not be so worried about how others view them. Of course, some people are shy and you don't want to make them feel bad, but you should be able to tell that before you test this out. The kind of person we're talking about is not shy – they love to be the center of attention, but only when they are in control.

7) Watch his driving behavior, especially when he is stuck in traffic. Does he speed a lot? Weave in and out of traffic? Yell, swear, call names or otherwise get excessively upset about being stopped in traffic? While most people can admit to getting frustrated and saying things about other drivers when traffic is bad, look for a consistent pattern of excessive anger in situations most people would handle with a simple shrug and a sigh and putting a good song on the radio.

Additionally, if he says or does anything to make you uncomfortable while driving, ask him politely to change it. "I really feel uncomfortable driving at this speed – could you please slow down for me?" Or, "I'd feel safer if we left a couple more car lengths when we're driving this fast." See how he responds. If he gets angry at you or ignores your requests, that's almost a sure sign that his ego will always trump your needs.

Remember again that not all Jerks come off as egotistical. Some are very clingy and needy and not at all competitive. And there are some men with somewhat inflated egos that can still be OK as partners. But don't bet on it. Excessive competitiveness and the need to put on a good show are definitely red flags that your Jerk Radar should be attuned to. While it is a softer sign than some, it is also one of the first things you'll be able to notice as he gets more comfortable with you. So don't use it as the only signal, but if you see it, always look deeper – there may be more to this than a simple case of excess testosterone.

CHAPTER 5

Isolation/Intensity of Involvement

I MET MY EX AND THE NEXT NIGHT HE TURNED UP AT MY DOOR. WE LIVED an hour and a half drive away from each other and he turned up every night, after work, for a week. He was charming, saying things like I was the most beautiful girl in world. He said he told his best mate, the night he met me, that he was going to marry me. He made me feel like the only woman that ever mattered to him. After 1 week, he proposed, saying he wanted to marry me and couldn't live without me. We waited another 5 weeks before we told my parents. During these five weeks he spent every spare minute with me.... He was charming, funny, and I felt like I was the only thing that ever mattered to him.

—AS, 56, , Australia, 13-year abusive marriage

Isolation is one of the almost universal tactics of any abusive person. This is for one main reason: the more isolated you are from others, the harder it is for you to check your reality and his statements with others who can verify that he is up to no good. So watching for attempts to isolate is one of the best ways to screen for Jerky tendencies. Unfortunately, it's not always obvious that isolation is happening, because it is presented in the context of intensity of love. The reasons given for isolation will almost always relate to how much he loves you. This may not even be said, but will be implied in his actions: he just wants to spend every second together with you – he can't stand for you to be apart.

Mark worked this way on Jan – he created a lot of special trips and dinners out and intense sexuality, cleverly combined with "supportive" comments about how unfairly her parents (whom she lived with) treated her. He worked to set up an intense, whirlwind romance where she had little time for anything but work and him. This set the stage for an early request for her to move in with him, a request she wisely refused.

As in every one of these early indicators, a desire for intensity and constant companionship may not be a problem in itself – some people are just like that. If it's the only sign, it's probably because the person is in love and is getting a little obsessed with you. In this case, setting a few limits on the person's intensity may hurt his feelings a bit, but he will understand and back off if you need some space. A true Jerk, on the other hand, will continue to press himself forward and not give up until he has got you on his terms.

Very Quick Involvement

So what does isolation look like early in a relationship? The first sign is a desire for very quick involvement to a high level of intimacy. The Jerk will often move from a dinner date to "I love you" to "Let's move in together" in a matter of weeks, sometimes even days. This is not a sign that you've found your soul mate – it is more likely an attempt to create a haze of intense romance so thick that you won't see or think beyond the immediate moment.

> He moved in fast and quick, asking for a commitment – he loved me, did I love him? When I said he was moving quickly, he'd say "I was a Marine, Marines do things quickly." We were married 7 months after we met.
>
> –L, USA, 40, 11-year abusive relationship

This is one of those areas where our media picture of "romance" works against us. So many romantic movies represent love as something that comes at you all of a sudden, and sweeps you off your feet in an irresistible wave of emotion. He is "The One!" There's nothing you can to do hold it back, because it's destiny! Your perfect man has met his perfect woman, and you will live and love happily ever after, just like in the fairy tales and movies we talked about in Chapter 2.

Unfortunately, your Jerky partner has watched these movies, too, and knows how to play this game. Some do it very consciously as a means of conquering you, while others simply do it without thinking because that's what seems to work for them. But conscious or not, the intense involvement is part of the play to get you to drop all your other friends and activities and devote all of your energies towards this new and wonderful relationship that is going to make your life complete. There is no need at this stage to tell you not to see your friends or family. The path is to make things so wonderful and romantic and intense that you don't even want to do anything but spend time with him.

This is the "honeymoon period" you may have heard about, where the abusive person puts you on a pedestal – you can do no wrong, you are beautiful, you are special, you are the only one for him, he never loved another person like you, he can't live without you, and on and on. There may be intense emotion, even tears, frequently some intense sexual attraction, and it can feel very, very good to you. Especially if you are a person who grew up being treated badly or being ignored, this may be the first time you ever felt beautiful, special, smart, interesting, or whatever feelings this person evokes in you. He may very well seem like the best thing that ever happened to you. He is the perfect man!

> ... he won my heart, and part of his winning was a wonderful sexual experience in the first few days. He was 9 years younger than me and he had a history of violence

and verbal abuse, but I didn't know it. He swept me off my feet in those first weeks and when I orgasmed, it was better than ever before, and I was 32 years old! He was attentive sexually and seemed to want me all the time – every night, and I was a bit overweight and self-conscious, but it didn't seem to bother him. My pleasure was the most important thing he had to do – for 6 weeks. That was when he knew I was madly in love with him, as he said he was with me, but he started changing and being abrasive and not so tender.

–SM, 65 now, 35 then, Indiana, married 22 years

Of course, it's normal when feeling "in love" to spend a lot of time with your partner. But it's also normal to take some time to get to know each other before making a total commitment. There are certainly legitimate tales of "love at first sight." It is rare but does happen, as it did for my parents.

But when your partner wants to spend every second together, when other friends and family are forgotten, when you start being late for work, or he calls you so often during work that your boss complains, or you are losing lots of sleep because the two of you are together every minute of the day, it's time to take a breath and get some perspective.

He would follow me around right from when he met me and make sure he was at the same bars, etc. After we started going out only 2-3 times, he texted and called a lot, saying he just cared and liked me so much. I don't remember when he first said he loved me, but it was soon after we started dating.... He introduced me to his father very fast and offered me rides everywhere I would go. [He would] show up unexpectedly at my workplace, friends' places he wasn't invited to, or just drive down the road if he didn't know where I was and I had my phone off. He would pretend he was worried about my safety when I planned a trip with someone else and talk me into taking the trip later or with him instead. He made it sound like he just cared so much. He was all over me, my life and all aspects of it, presenting himself as a charming and caring guy…

—Anonymous, 24, Germany, 8 months in abusive relationship

Downgrading Friends and Family

There is usually a two-sided aspect of this phase – in addition to the intense efforts at charm and romance, there can be a subtle or sometimes not-so-subtle pressure for you to go along with his thinking or plans. You may start feeling you are neglecting your friends or your family, and he'll assure you they will be OK without you, or say that if they really cared about you, they wouldn't begrudge you happiness. He may subtly imply that certain friends or family are not really supportive of you, or make minor criticisms of them, or share things "he has heard" about people you care about. This is definitely a sign you don't want to overlook. Jerks will actually make things up or exaggerate stories or put the most negative spin on an incident to start you doubting people that you have trusted in the past. If he says something about a friend that you just don't think seems true, check it out with that person or someone who knows them. If you find he's been putting "spin" on events, it's time to run like hell. He's trying to isolate you by downgrading your friends and family so he will be the only person you trust.

He would always resent it when I had plans with my friend. At first, he'd say "Oh, you want to see her? But I had great plans for us for tonight. Please call her and say you can't come over. I want to be with you and I don't want to spend the evening alone. You can visit her another time, OK?" Then pretty soon it was "I don't think she's as good a friend to you as you claim. I think she's just using you for achieving her own goals, and doesn't really care about you." Then "Didn't I tell you that she's selfish and not trustworthy? You really ought to find better friends." In the end, it was "If you call her again, or meet her, please don't come back again."

–KK, 30, Estonia, 7-year abusive relationship

Schedule Conflicts

Another subtle way Jerks will isolate and intensify the relationship is to create unpredictable changes in plans or schedules. You may have something already planned with a friend or colleague, and he "just happens" to come up with concert tickets or a party or a plan to go out of town that simply can't wait. As always, this kind of thing can happen in any normal relationship. But a normal partner will understand that you have your own life and activities, and will either make efforts to plan around them, or will attend these events alone or with another friend if you can't come along, rather than try to talk you into going. They may be disappointed, but they can accept that you have a life outside of their sphere of interest and control. A Jerk, on the other hand, will attempt to pressure or manipulate you into changing your plans. He may plead, bargain, or even get a little "frustrated" with you, showing an edge of anger maybe for the first time, so you will get the idea that you don't want to disappoint him. And suddenly, you find yourself changing your plans and going along with him and not being quite sure how or why it happened. If this starts happening a lot, back off and take a more objective look at what is going on.

The conflicts may also happen with an odd frequency that suggests they are not entirely random. He may know that you have plans and be intentionally creating conflicts so you'll have to decide whether to go with him or not. This kind of testing is an indication of a very self-centered and manipulative person. If you get the feeling he is doing this to try and prevent you from having a life outside of your relationship, it's definitely time to look elsewhere. It's only going to go downhill from there.

> On many occasions, he has insisted I do something he plans despite me accepting invites ahead of time. Sometimes I've gone ahead and done my own thing, but it's like an act of congress getting him to "agree" to it.
>
> —Anonymous, 35, Vermont, 5-year abusive relationship

> Another trick was when I'd made arrangements to go out with friends, at the last minute, he'd have made plans to go out, knowing that I was due out but wouldn't leave the children on their own. He knew the children were my Achilles heel. And there was no thought of him changing his plans. It was always me who had to.
>
> —TR, 25-year abusive relationship

Unreasonable Jealousy

Jerks will often be unreasonably jealous of your contact with other people, especially anyone that could be a potential partner. He may ask you questions about what you do together, whether you feel attracted to a particular person, or may just get upset that you "see them so much." He may even say outright, jokingly or seriously, "You like him/her better than you like me." He may say that any woman who talks with another man is hitting on him. You may often feel compelled to reassure your partner that you are not looking for another man/woman, and yet despite all evidence, find that they are still suspicious. He may bring up his old girlfriend or ex-wife who cheated on him to explain why he's so sensitive. He may have other reasons or explanations.

You may want to chalk this up to insecurity on his part and figure that time will prove that you are true to him. But this kind of irrational jealousy is not good news. It can be either an intentional tactic to keep you isolated, or a warning sign that this person is obsessive and sees you as a possession. This is the kind of person who will stalk an ex-partner, and leaving such a person can be extremely dangerous, or in rare cases even fatal. Most of the murder-suicides you read about in the paper are perpetrated by just this kind of man. Obsessive jealousy or paranoia about you leaving for another partner is a big red flag that should never be ignored.

> He was jealous of my children. He would accuse me of loving them more than I love him. He was jealous of my mother, as a matter of fact he was jealous of everybody. If I spoke to somebody too long he would question me as to what I was talking about, that the person, man or woman, was flirting with me.
>
> –Anonymous

> He also would cause arguments if we had anyone round. If it was a friend of his, he'd be ok. But if it was a friend of mine, or a more mutual friend he'd start something.... He'd be mad at me afterwards, saying I was giggling too much, I was looking at the other person with "flirty eyes," or I looked them up and down, when I was just acting normal, or trying NOT to do those things on purpose.
>
> –JD

This is another place where movies and TV shows are not helping women stay safe. Jealousy is repeatedly reflected as a sign of love. There's nothing quite so romantic in film as two boys or men fighting over the girl they love. As a result, you may feel flattered and attractive when your new man is willing to fight for you. It's right out of Robin Hood! It can feel very exciting to be the "damsel in distress."

Unfortunately, in reality, this kind of jealousy does not reflect love so much as a belief that a girlfriend is a POSSESSION, and that the winner of a fight can claim her as a prize. It also shouldn't be too much of a stretch to see that a person who would beat someone else up (or threaten to) over you is also more likely to use violence to solve other problems, including problems within a relationship. While this kind of behavior is culturally supported and may emerge in any male who is feeling their power threatened, a pattern of this kind of jealous behavior is not a sign of love. It's a sign of self-centeredness and obsession.

You may see it as a man's role to protect you from danger. This can be a legitimate traditional way of assuring your safety, especially if you live in or are traveling in a place that is dangerous. But a true gentleman will be fighting to defend YOUR honor, not his own. He will not leap to conclusions or start a conflict over innocent behavior. He'll respect your right to talk with anyone, male or female, and will only intervene if your safety is genuinely threatened. This is very different from a partner getting upset with someone for talking to you, or starting an argument with someone who compliments your appearance or appears to be admiring you from across the room. And any partner who gets upset with *you* for reaching out to talk with people in your community, regardless of their gender, is someone who does not respect you as a human being.

I have been alone in a number of cities on business, and have met with female friends and colleagues there. My wife knew all about these meetings and never had a concern. Similarly, she has had lunches or other meetings with male coworkers or friends and I never gave it a second thought. We have a level of trust in each other that means we don't have to worry about the other person being unfaithful. This should be the direction a healthy relation-ship is heading in, rather than one of restriction and paranoia. You shouldn't have to spend your time reassuring your partner you're not sleeping around. If you do, there is something desperately wrong, most likely with him.

> If I was not home when he called I was out sleeping around. He went to jail for a third DUI, and if I was not there to accept his call I was sleeping around. As a

> matter of fact I could be shopping with the kids and take
> too long and I was sleeping around. We moved to the
> country, and I was left all day with no car and no means
> to go out. He would in the winter check to see if there
> were strange tire tracks in the snow. In the summer he
> would see if the gravel in the lane was moved in any way.
> If it was, I was having people over during the day and
> having an affair.
>
> —Anonymous

This kind of behavior is particularly disturbing early on in a relationship. If you have known someone a couple of weeks, what right do they have to expect that you will be "dating exclusively," let alone to be screening your friends and companions for sexual intent? It's absolutely outrageous to expect "loyalty" in a dating relationship unless there is some explicit agreement of exclusiveness between you.

And even if there is such an agreement, he should trust you to keep your word. If he's doubting your integrity, unless you really are a sneaky and duplicitous Jerk yourself, it generally means he doesn't put much stock in promises and agreements. It most likely indicates that he's lacking integrity himself and expects you to be just as sneaky and deceptive as he is. In fact, an unfounded fear of a partner's infidelity is often an indication that he is prone to infidelity himself and assumes you will do the same to him. If he can't trust you to keep your word, there's not much point in having a relationship at all, at least in my book. Trust is the core of a relationship. A person who can't trust you can't love you in a mature way, either. But they sure can work their butts off controlling everything you do.

> I was athletic and always on a volleyball team year round
> with my friend and all her brothers (she had 6 of them);
> we would all hang out and have a great time. Of course,
> he had to join the team also, saying that he knew how

to play (he was terrible). Now I know he joined to watch over me with all those boys. He would start saying things like, "You shouldn't hang out with them by yourself if you have a boyfriend," or he would say, "I can see that they have a crush on you..." He said that something could happen, [so] I shouldn't hang out with them. I also had a male friend at work that he forbade me to go to lunch with alone. If I went out to lunch he'd always be quick to ask who all went.

–L, USA, 40, 11-year abusive relationship

Fast Commitment

Which leads to the "commitment" question. Abusers very often ask for and expect commitment very early in a relationship. They may be telling you how wonderful you are and how they can't imagine how they ever lived without you, but at the same time, they'll be directly or indirectly suggesting that you ought to feel the same way. He may ask for you to be "exclusive" way before you are ready for this. He may ask to move into your home or ask you to move in with him within days or weeks of knowing you. He may immediately want to meet your kids and spend time "as a family" even though he barely knows you. He may want you to have the kids call him "daddy." He may even propose marriage in a very romantic and seemingly sincere manner.

While all of this may feel flattering to you, it is really quite abnormal and almost always indicates someone who is interested in gaining control over you. He wants you to make a commitment before he could possibly know that the relationship will be workable. He wants you to adopt him into your family before you have any sense of who he really is or how he'll fit in. He wants you to give up your independence as a sign of your devotion to him and to your relationship. DON'T DO IT!

He said he loved me and proposed on the first date. Why did I not run screaming!!!!

–SK, 46, USA

We had been dating for about two weeks, and had been out maybe 4 or 5 times…when he produced a necklace with a heart shaped pendant from his pocket. [He said] he wanted me to wear it all the time. He was just that into me and had never ever met anyone even remotely as smart and beautiful and fun as me and he knew he wanted to spend the rest of his life with me. This after dating for 2 weeks!

The next week, he took me to his mother's place to introduce me to her, saying that it was important to him that his mother meet the girl he was gonna marry and have a family with.

–KK, 30, Estonia, 7-year abusive relationship

It is proper to be very skeptical of anyone who wants a fast commitment. In my experience, it indicates a shallowness and a superficial sense of what a relationship is all about. A person who truly understands and wants closeness and intimacy will know that you can't establish a real, trusting relationship in just a few days or weeks. Sure, you can have an intense and fun and sexy and exciting time, but it is just the beginning of getting to know each other. Just like kids who don't know a stranger are naturally cautious, you should always be wary of a new partner who wants to get too close too fast. At best, is a sure sign of immaturity and self-centeredness. At worst, it could be the first indication that you are about to connect with someone whose version of love is to suck the life energy right out of you until you have nothing left to give.

As always, it's important to recognize that some people are just spontaneous and believe things will work out. Such people do exist and are not necessarily immature or shallow. But the proper response is to slow things down. A person who genuinely cares about you will understand your desire to get to know him before committing to anything more serious. He will understand that you may be in a different place than he is and will adjust his expectations accordingly. But the true Jerk will simply continue the pressure to get really close, really fast and will not give up until he has accomplished his objective. If you are also one of those spontaneous people, this may be extremely challenging for you to implement. But if you want to keep from having yet another Jerk take advantage of you, slow is the way to go.

Rapid Sexual Involvement

A word here about sexuality. One of the cardinal signs of a Jerk is the desire for rapid sexual involvement. I grew up in the days of the "sexual revolution" and understand and fully support a woman's right to sexual freedom and enjoyment. But I have to say, as restrictive as the old mores were, there is a lot to be said for delaying sexual activity in a relationship. It's a great way to tell what a person is about. Setting sexual boundaries early in the relationship can show you what a person's motivations really are. If you move very slowly, a person with sexual preoccupations will be unable to resist pressuring you to go further than you have indicated is comfortable for you.

> He insisted on an exclusive relationship when I was not ready. He wanted sex on the first date. I said forget it. Eventually, we did get sexual, and then he said he could not have sex with me and [allow me to] date other people (although I was not).
>
> –TK, 59, Canada, 10-year abusive relationship

Any sense that you are being pressured to get involved sexually more quickly than you are comfortable is something to be VERY concerned about. Listen for guilt trips, complaints, implications that other women have gone further sooner, suggestions that your love needs to "go to the next level," or anything other than a simple discussion of your needs and feelings. If you find yourself worrying that if you don't give in to his requests or demands, he will leave you for someone else, then you are almost certainly being manipulated.

Of course, you may also have the belief, which is not uncommon these days, that you have to be sexual early to "hold onto your man." There are a lot of messages in society that suggest that men who don't get sex early in a relationship will look elsewhere.

I absolutely agree that this is true for some men. But those are the Jerks! Those are *exactly* the men you WANT to have looking elsewhere! Any suggestion that you use your sexuality to keep a man around who would otherwise leave is demeaning to your value as a human being and as a woman. A man should want to be with you because he likes your company. Sexual attraction is part of that scenario, but attraction doesn't mean you have to have sex right away. Get to know him first and see how he does with delayed gratification. If sex is his main objective, you'll start to see the signs or pressure or manipulation, and you'll know you have a Jerk on your hands. And if he decides to look elsewhere because you won't "put out," be happy you got rid of him as fast as you did, because he didn't deserve you in the first place.

> We made love on the first night we met, I didn't want to but felt like I had no choice and didn't think I would see him again anyway.
>
> —AS, 56, Australia, 13-year abusive marriage

Pregnancy and Birth Control

Another way that Jerks demand or arrange for rapid commitment is through pregnancy. They may pressure you relatively early in a relationship to have a baby together. This may happen before you're sure of the relationship, or before you have the finances to manage a baby, or before you are married (if that's important to you), or before you are emotionally ready. They may "accept" your first response but continue to bring up the issue, and may subtly imply that your love or your confidence in him or the relationship must be weak or you'd be willing to go through with it. If a baby was not in your plans and he is trying to get you to change your mind, especially when it's early in a relationship, this indicates a total disrespect for your boundaries. The odds are good that he doesn't actually want to have a child, but wants you to be pregnant because it will create greater dependency on him, thereby giving him more control over you.

> [She] refused to give me "space", and I felt smothered and that I was being rail-roaded all the time: into marriage, into moving home, into buying a "family" car despite having no intent of having a family, even having that family...
>
> –CB, male, 49, UK, 17-year abusive relationship

Even worse is the birth control manipulation. I have heard more than one case where the abuser (male or female) sabotaged birth control efforts in order to create a pregnancy. This is something you've probably heard of for women, claiming they are on birth control and then getting pregnant in order to force someone to marry them. But I have seen it the other way as well. My favorite example is how Larry hooked Annie into getting pregnant – he assured her he'd become sterile due to exposure to radiation in the military. I am sure he was just "shocked" when he discovered she got pregnant – "I guess those incompetent doctors screwed us both over again." Except the doctors probably never said anything of the kind – he wanted her to get pregnant so he could control her more effectively.

Another approach is the old "I can't enjoy sex with a condom" routine. Or "I'm so horny right now, I just can't wait." There are many variations on this theme, but the idea is that you feel pressured to be irresponsible about birth control so that you "accidentally" or intentionally get pregnant, which fits in with the Jerk's plans to get you committed early and completely to his control game.

Soon after we were engaged he told me to stop taking birth control because he wanted to have a child and we might as well start trying. Now that I think of it, it was probably a tactic to keep me from leaving him before the wedding. Though I gave him no reasons to think I would have done that.

—Anonymous, 35, Vermont, 5-year abusive relationship

Pressure to Move In Together

The other favorite routine is the pressure to move in together. This is one of the most common strategies, and is genuinely hard to detect. This is because couples moving in together has become rather routine in our culture. There are a lot of accepted arguments, such as the idea that if we move in together, we can test out and see if the relationship will really work. While this sounds like a reasonable argument, in the mouth of a Jerk, it can be a strong manipulative tool to increase his control. For one thing, once you are moved in together, he'll have a lot more opportunities to plant seeds of doubt in you. He can make comments to help you doubt your friends, your family, your intelligence, your appearance, your sexual performance, your competence, all in the guise of "helpful feedback."

But just as important, once he's in, it's a lot harder to get rid of him. You start buying things together, arranging rooms as a couple, planning dinners, trips, spending, and entertainment together, merging finances into a joint account, having his name on the bills or the lease or the mortgage, loaning each other money, sharing vehicles – in short, he now has a great deal of control over a lot of areas of your life, and to escape will become very much more complicated. A Jerk who is interested in long-term abuse rather than a quick fling will frequently want to move in with you early in the relationship. It is not a sign of commitment. It's a sign of a need for control and a desire to create that early commitment from you that will be hard to back out of once his true Jerkiness starts to show through. Don't do it!

Moving Away to Be with Him

The next step is convincing you to move somewhere else to be together, just the two of you. Again, very romantic and accepted in our culture, and of course, there are certainly legitimate reasons for moving and wanting someone to come with you. But if the move seems sudden or unplanned, or it seems very early in a relationship to consider such a move, it may be a tactical maneuver. Will you have to give up your job? Will it mean moving away from friends and family? And what is the purpose of moving – does he really have a position in another location that he needs to move to for career advancement or to keep his job? Or is it just a theoretical opportunity that could be bogus? Does he understand and appreciate the difficulties this would involve for you? Is he willing to consider a long-distance relationship or look for other potential solutions to this problem of geographical separation?

Moving to another place for a partner is a very big decision. It should not be entered into lightly, and it should be clearly understood that there will be challenges to be faced. It should also be your decision whether or not to go, without pressure from him. It's always an option to have a long-distance relationship. There are even married people who have to live in different cities for a while in order for each partner and the family to be able to best meet their needs. Any such decision should be yours and should be made by honest review of the pros and cons, with all options on the table. If the "only way" is for you to move with him, if he is upset that you have considerations, if he starts to suggest that maybe you don't really care about him if you don't move, it is a definite sign of danger.

Jerks want you to move to be with them because if you do, you lose your support system. It's part of the isolation plan, and it can be extremely effective. This is especially true if you are moving to a place you are unfamiliar with but where he has connections and knowledge of the community. It's hard enough to break into a new community without having someone undermining your attempts to get settled, but that's just what a Jerk will do once you get to where he wants you. He will work hard to assure that your only connections are ones that he wants you to have, and that you are as dependent on him for survival as he can arrange. This is what happened to Annie. Once she was a continent away from her support system, and dependent on him for shelter and food for her and her baby, it was very difficult for her to get away, and Larry had a lot of control over her life.

> My Ex was in the army so we moved around a lot and in doing this I was kept away from family and friends.
>
> **−AS, 56, Australia, 13-year abusive marriage**

Before you ever consider such a move, even with a person who seems otherwise fine, make very certain you have plans to connect and create a support system in the new environment. If there are ANY other red flags, even just one, DO NOT MOVE to accommodate your partner's needs! If it's meant to be, you will be able to tolerate time apart and the challenges of separation will solidify your trust and confidence in the relationship. But if he is a Jerk, he will not quietly let you stay behind. And if he cancels his plans after pressuring you to come along and finding out you won't, I'd be very concerned that he was making up the "plans" to get you under his control.

> He got a job in Dubai in 2003 and wanted me to go with him he made it sound so good.... We got married in 2003 he left to Dubai a week later and I was devastated to be apart from him...
>
> Once we got abroad the isolation was worse – he would take my mobile away from me and then in the

morning play a game with me about where he had hidden it ie – hot or cold – and eventually I would get it back. He would call me all day to know what I was doing...

–Anonymous, UK

Controlling Communication

A big part of isolation is control of communication. Frequent calls at work may be a sign that he is very attached to you. They can also be an indicator of a desire to check up on you and make sure you get used to it. Frequently erased messages that your partner "forgot to tell you about" could be a sign of an absent-minded person. But they could also indicate an attempt to undermine your connections with other friends and family. Asking about who you were just talking to might suggest a benign interest in your life. Or it might suggest that he's checking up on who you're talking to and why. Covert monitoring of calls or e-mails is a definite sign of Jerkiness, and would be a deal-breaker for me. And any person who tells you that you have to be somewhere and they will call you to make sure you are there is a stalker looking for a victim.

No one should monitor or control your communications. You have a right to talk to anyone you want to and don't need to tell him about it. If he says that you not telling him means you don't trust him, he's trying to make you feel guilty for having a sense of privacy. And besides, why should you trust him if he won't trust you to talk to people without checking up on you? Even in the closest of relationships, people don't share everything. And I am betting that he would not feel compelled to tell you who he's with or where he's going all the time, nor would you probably ever need or want to know. It's not normal to track your partner's activities that closely, unless you have some ulterior motive. In this case, the motive is to gain more control of your communications and to manipulate you into believing that you have to check in with him constantly.

Certainly, I am not saying that finding out where your partner

is going and when they'll be back is a sign of evil intent, especially if you are living together. For practical reasons, it's sometimes necessary to get a sense of what's happening so you can plan your day or evening. And you may be interested in hearing about friends if a partner is inclined to share. What I'm talking about is a constant prying, a need to know all the time, in detail, what you're doing and who you are doing it with. This is often accompanied by strange or inexplicable accusations or fears – you are having an affair, you are leaving him, etc.

> He emailed me incessantly. He called me frequently. He flirted with me outrageously. He was frantic if I was five minutes late even just calling him – saying he thought I might have been mugged or something. I loved the attention. Wow, did he ever care!!
>
> Then, wham – he forbade me to even have coffee in broad daylight three blocks from his house with an old boyfriend and his five year old son.
>
> –TK, 59, Canada, 10-year abusive relationship

> He always wanted to know where I was going and to be honest, not telling him wasn't worth it, so abusive would he be. He also wanted to know what friends were going to be there, and then it would be the Spanish Inquisition when I got home – who was there, who said what, etc.
>
> –TR, 25-year abusive relationship

If you find you can't go anywhere without getting the third degree, or that you are unfairly accused of infidelity, or simply of abandoning him because you "just don't care," if you find you are feeling the need to explain or defend yourself when doing something simple like going for a walk or visiting a friend or family member, stop and take a look what's going on. Why should you have to explain or justify your contact with the world? Why should he be worried that you are sleeping with the neighbor every time

you take the dog for a walk? These are not normal fears. They either reflect a paranoid, controlling kind of personality, who will never rest easy unless you are in their sight, or they indicate a manipulative strategy to keep you away from other people who might interfere with his nefarious plans. Either way, you have a sure-fire Jerk on your hands if they want to control your contacts and communication in this way.

Stopping Your Career

The last point I'll mention in this section is regarding your career. Some Jerks, but definitely not all, will not want you to work. They may go back to the old "traditional roles" argument, saying that the man should earn money and take care of the woman, that you shouldn't have to work, that you should be able to stay home with the kids, and so forth. This could be totally legitimate for some men – they just grew up that way and think it would be better for you not to have to work. But it is often another isolation tactic, an effort to keep you away from other people who could help you keep perspective on what is going on. The important part here is for you to maintain your integrity. If you want to stay home with the kids and your partner is willing to "bring home the bacon," that's great! You are coming to an agreement that meets both of your needs as well as the kids' needs.

But if you would really prefer to work or to advance your skills through education and he wants you to stop, find out exactly why. If he is threatened by you working, this is a very bad sign. Why should that be threatening? What kind of insecurity would make it difficult for him to accept that you want to work? Does he feel bad that you might earn more money than him? Why shouldn't you? Does he complain that "you spend most of your income on daycare?" Well, if that's what works for you, what is wrong with that? The big question to ask yourself is, "whose needs are being met by his proposed arrangement?" If the answer is that it meets

only his needs, then he should be completely willing for you to have a different plan than his. It's not your job to rearrange your life to meet his needs. Anyone who thinks differently is a Jerk with a capital "J"!

PREVENTING ISOLATION

So how do you check someone out for isolationist tendencies? Here are some ideas:

1) **First and foremost, *always* move slowly in a relationship.** Even if you really feel good about the relationship, take your time and progress at a pace that feels comfortable to you, or even slower than you think necessary if you have a tendency to jump into things yourself. If you find you are spending every minute together, take a break and make some plans to do something alone or with friends.

This has two positive effects: first, it enables you to back up and get some perspective on how things are going without the intensity of the moment to distract you. Second, it gives you a chance to see how he reacts to you doing your own thing. If taking some time alone or seeing your friends creates problems for him, you are probably better off letting him go, even if things seemed promising. Normal people have friends and activities outside of their primary relationship. If he doesn't like that, he's going to be big trouble down the line.

2) **Delay sexual involvement** (unless you're just looking for a fling yourself). One of the surest ways to detect a sexual predator is to refuse his advances. Normal partners won't press once they know your boundaries. Those who do most likely have sexual conquest as one of their main relationship objectives. As much as this pressuring behavior is socially accepted, I don't think it is at all healthy, and the sooner you find out this is where he's coming from, the

better off you'll be. You may be accused of being "old fashioned," but you'll be a lot safer and more confident if you decide the time is right without pressure from your partner. When in doubt, wait it out. His reaction will tell you a lot about who he really is.

3) Try challenging early declarations of love that seem too quick to be real. "Wow, we've known each other for two weeks and have seen each other only five times. Doesn't it seem a little early to talk about love?" Or more humorously, "I bet you say that to all the girls." Or how about, "Well, I appreciate you sharing your feelings, but it's way too early for me to be talking about love. We barely know each other. Let's take our time and not rush things." These are reasonable statements that should cool things off a bit if the person is just being excessively romantic or overenthusiastic. For a Jerk on the prowl, though, such statements will usually provoke one of two reactions: either he'll agree with you in theory, but revert back to that behavior in a couple of days (or hours or minutes), or he will try to convince you that he really does love you that much no matter what you say.

Try to be objective in watching his reaction. If he's trying really hard to convince you that you have already earned his undying devotion in the few short days you have known him, if he's using terms like "soul mate" or "forever" way too early and won't back down, don't buy into it. If this is his only flaw, you may forgive it, but be alert for other red flags, because most of the time, mature people understand that love is something that develops over time. Don't fall for the romance – test him out and see how he handles you putting on the brakes.

4) Resist any attempts to get an early commitment from you that you're not comfortable with. Whether it's sex, exclusive dating, moving in together, marriage, or having a baby, if you don't feel 100% comfortable, say NO. If he really loves you, he'll respect your right to make up your own mind in your own time. If you feel ANY pressure to change your mind after you've made yourself

clear, I'd say it's a deal-breaker. You don't want to be with someone who wants you to commit out of guilt or fear. Anyone who wants such a commitment is more interested in control than in love.

5) In any relationship, intentionally set aside some time to be alone or to spend with friends, and make sure he knows that's what you are doing. Watch for signs of jealousy, or subtle attempts to discourage you from spending time in ways you have always found helpful or enjoyable (including those "conflicts" that he may be intentionally creating). Make sure you continue your hobbies or outside groups, and if he tries to stop you, put on the brakes quickly. A person who really cares about you will want you to do things that make you happy. Rather than talking you out of your weekly soccer match or your bridge group, he'll either come and watch you play or find something else to do with his time. Any attempts to discourage you from living your own life should be taken very, very seriously. Remember that abuse is about control, not violence, and one of the earliest signs of control is trying to decide what you do with your time and whom you hang out with.

Also watch out if he wants to join every group you're in and be "with you" in all your activities. You need some separate time, and if he can't allow that, he will start allowing less and less freedom as time goes on.

6) Immediately challenge any attempts, no matter how gentle or subtle, to put down your friends or family. He's welcome to share his own feelings and impressions, but when he tries to tell you what to think and feel, he's out of line. Let him know right up front, calmly but firmly, that you'll make your own decisions about whom you like and don't like, and that you don't appreciate any meddling in your affairs. If he continues, or if he tries to defend his actions as "just trying to help you out," watch out! Trying to control your connections to friends or family is a very bad sign. It's rare that a Jerk will come right out and say, "I don't want you seeing your Aunt Minnie" (at least, not until they have a lot more

control over you), but the first sign of control in this area is the general put-down. Don't tolerate it for a minute!

7) If you find he has a lot of surprise plans, try not going along with him a couple of times. If you had something planned, tell him you're sorry to miss out, but you have commitments. Or if you just don't feel like it, let him know you're not in the mood and see what he does. If a person surprises you with a plan, they really have no right to expect you to go along. That's the risk of a surprise – the person may or may not like it. If he can't accept that you're not in the mood or have other plans, you're going to run into a lot of trouble down the line when your agenda and his conflict. This is an early indication that he needs to have his way despite your needs and feelings, and that's a sure sign you want to look for greener pastures.

8) Watch for any signs of unusual or irrational jealousy. You should be able to hang out with your friends without an accounting of whom you were with or what you were doing. Listen for any implication that you are cheating on him or that by being with someone else, you're saying they're more important than he is. Jealous feelings toward old boyfriends are also suspect. Remember that jealousy generally denotes possessiveness. Unless you are openly flirting with someone or actually sleeping with someone else behind his back (assuming you have agreed to be exclusive, otherwise, have at it!), he really has no reason to be jealous. He does not own you, and you have a right to have friends and experiences that don't involve him. If he can't handle that, you don't want him in your life.

9) Consider any suggestion that you move in order to be with him with the utmost caution. Move ONLY because you think it is best for you. Any attempts to guilt-trip, manipulate, or argue you into going along with his plan to move you are a BIG red flag and should start a total re-thinking of your relationship. This is

particularly the case if you have not been together very long, or if the job prospect or reason for him moving is speculative, or if it would mean losing your support network and moving to a place where he is at home. I am not saying no one should ever move to accommodate a partner, but this kind of move is a real commitment and should never be entered into lightly. Any effort to make you feel bad about thinking over your options is a very, very bad sign.

10) Any attempt to control your communication should be immediately confronted head on. If you are being asked to check in at regular intervals, to be somewhere at a certain time if he calls, to explain yourself if you were out with friends, or to reassure him that you are not sleeping with someone else, you are definitely going out with a Jerk. Same if he is checking your e-mails or cell phone or other communication. Let him know in no uncertain terms that you will NOT be allowing him to keep tabs on you, not now or ever. If he denies this behavior, or minimizes it, or comes up with excuses, or blames you in any way for him spying, deleting messages, or checking up on you, GET GOING NOW! You do not need to explain or justify your connections with other human beings or activities. If you find yourself feeling like you have to do so, the odds are overwhelming that you are being manipulated.

11) Maintain your employment, volunteer work, or schooling if you want to. If he has objections, ask him to explain why you should stop doing what you were already doing before he met you. If he loves you the way you are, he should support you in doing things that you already like or need to do. If he tries to pressure you to change your activities to accommodate him, ask yourself, "Where will this process stop?" Make it clear early on that you won't stop anything that you do because of him. If he can't handle it, let him walk. You will be saving yourself a lot of trouble later on.

In summary, a big push for quick commitment and intimacy is often the first indication that your partner wants to control your every action. Assert your rights early and often, including your right to do as you wish and associate with whomever you please without his permission. Let him know you won't be pressured into letting him make decisions for you. If he has a hard time accepting that, give him his walking papers early on. As exciting as it may seem, a lightning romance is almost a sure indication that you are being conned. Put the brakes on and see what happens. I know it's not romantic, but it's a lot safer in the long run.

CHAPTER 6

Irresponsibility/Lying

EARLY IN THEIR RELATIONSHIP, LARRY OFFERED ANNIE A LARGE AMOUNT of money to help keep her mother's house out of foreclosure. Annie was floored by this and tried several times to decline, but Larry was quite insistent. When she said she couldn't pay it back, he said it was a gift to her and she didn't have to worry about it. Months later, he insisted that she pay him back, seeming to "forget" that he had told her it was a gift. When she tried to remind him of this, he accused her of lying and trying to take advantage of his kindness in "loaning" her the money.

If you were looking for a universal characteristic among the various types of Jerks in the world, this one would be the best choice. Abusive people are irresponsible. They blame others for their own choices, they minimize the negative impact of their own behavior, and they expect to be bailed out for free when they get into trouble. When they are in trouble, they'll promise you the moon, but they just can't seem to find a way to follow through on their agreements. A Jerk may or may not charm or romance you, he may or may not control your phone calls, he may or may not try to get you to move in with him in a week, he may or may not brag or name drop, but you can count on the fact that he'll have a hard time keeping agreements or accepting the blame for anything that goes wrong.

Lying

Part of irresponsibility is lying. Jerks will lie and swear to it with a straight face when they have to protect their own interests, or sometimes just for the fun of fooling you. And since nothing is ever their fault, they will almost always be unable to make any genuine change that lasts longer than necessary to get you or the boss or the police off their backs. Which means you can't trust anything they say.

We saw a good example of media support for this behavior in Chapter 2 in the movie, *Only You*. We saw that our main character, Marisa Tomei, was lied to and deceived multiple times by the character played by Robert Downey, Jr., and yet ended up committed to him in the end. Downey certainly showed himself to be highly dishonest and irresponsible, but his boyish charm and the winds of fate made everything turn out OK.

> When I first met R in March 2008, he told me he was 37, the same age as me – he said that he had a very hard life! He told me that he had no "kiddies" and that his wife had died very tragically. He also lied about his first name (said it was R) and his last name! He also lied about his ethnic origin…he said that he was Italian mixed with Argentinian with a little English!
>
> One day whilst we were going for a walk, not that long after, he told me his real name which was K! He said that no one ever called him that and he hated that name. He also said that he didn't have any little ones but he had a grown up daughter ! Imagine my shock! She is now 32!!! He also said that his surname wasn't the Italian one…his dad is bog standard English, nothing else…. I was shocked and hurt that he could lie to me and all my thoughts were at that time was alarm bells, he is a liar! Run away! But, by then, he had got his hook deep inside me! He also told me that he was 50, not 37!… His excuse was that he didn't trust anyone, so he never gave

personal details out to any stranger…but by this point, we had become so close and he had already indicated he wanted to spend his life with me!

–AG, 40, England, UK

"Misunderstandings"

Another form of dishonesty is the "misunderstanding. This may not be obvious at the beginning when he's "charming" you, but give it a while and you'll start to see it showing. For example, he may start coming late to appointments with you. He'll apologize but be late to another meeting soon. Then, he'll start suggesting that maybe you got the time wrong. You will find yourself doubting your own recollections, because he'll be so certain and genuine in his denial. Next, he starts "remembering" your conversations differently, especially when it comes to anything he agreed to. "I never said I'd buy groceries today." "No, I told you I would be working late, you weren't listening." "I said I was coming by tonight, don't you remember?" Somehow, all of these little "misunderstandings" seem to involve YOU misunderstanding what HE supposedly said. It may seem like he believes what he's saying, but the truth is, he knows what you said and is lying to cover for his own irresponsibility.

His lies tended to be about small things, but were an absolute constant throughout the relationship until in the end, I never believed a word he said. He would lie about the most ridiculous things. For example, I might ask if he'd fed the dog, to which he'd say yes. Half an hour later the dog would come to me, I'd follow him and he'd lead me to his bowl which would indicate he hadn't been fed, so I'd ask my husband again and he'd say no, he hadn't fed him. I'd ask if he'd rung his parents and he'd say yes. I might then speak to them a few days later and mention that my husband had rung them, and they'd say

> no, he hadn't, so I'd check with my husband again and he'd say no, he hadn't rung them.
>
> —TR, abused 25 years

> He told me his dad wanted us to move to his house and was waiting for us.... A few months later his dad asks me when our vacation was over and when we were leaving, and I said I was told you invited us to move in…
>
> —KC

If you start feeling that sense of unreality around him a lot, like you have to keep checking your own memory to see if you somehow got it wrong, he's probably manipulating you. It may be very subtle at first, and slowly increase to the point that you really lose your own certainty and start wondering if you are losing your mind. If you get this feeling, stop and check out what is going on. Unless you are generally very forgetful with everyone, or have a hard time understanding what is said to you, why would you suddenly lose your memory capacity only with him? And why is it you that's always got it wrong? Couldn't he have made a mistake?

This is an early indication of low responsibility – an inability to ever be wrong. Normal people admit to shortcomings and recognize their strengths and weaknesses. They're able to allow that they are not perfect and may sometimes recall things differently than you. And their response to a lack of agreement is more likely to be to check their own recollection, rather than always assuming they recall with absolute certainty every time. A person who can't be wrong can't learn, and is going to be a problem to have around.

> [He] gave me the feeling something was unreal, and I really started to question if something was completely wrong with me or not – starting to wonder if my memory was wrong, if i drank too much maybe and did horrible things, etc.
>
> —Anonymous, 24, Germany, abused 8 months

Spotty Job History

Another sign of low responsibility is a spotty job history. Sure, some folks just like to change jobs a lot, but if you find that your partner is quitting jobs or being fired due to conflicts with the boss, you will want to look further into the reasons for this. Everybody probably has gotten fired once or twice in his/her life, or left a job that was a bad fit without having something lined up. But repeated job failures, long periods of unemployment, and difficulty getting along with supervisors are all signs of a person who is unable to handle conflict. The most likely reason is because he does things wrong and blames others for it, or gets into an argument when confronted. It may also indicate a difficulty keeping his word or following through with agreements, which are the cardinal signs of irresponsible behavior. A Jerk's job history will often tell you things about him you won't see when he's putting his "nice" face on for you. Get the straight scoop on any partner – check out his work history and see what it says about his level of responsibility.

Playing the Victim

Related to this is the Jerk's tendency to see himself as a victim in every difficult situation. Ask him about how he lost Job A – you will find that the boss was an ass, or they fired him due to reverse discrimination, or someone lied about him and blamed him for something he didn't do. Any of these things could happen once, or maybe twice. But if EVERY job he lost was someone else's fault, there is a problem. Even if the boss really was a Jerk, lots of us manage to deal with Jerky bosses and still not get fired. What did he do that contributed? What does he think he could have done differently to make the situation better? This kind of question can tell you a lot. Listen for signs of blame and a victim attitude. Responsible people try to look at their own behavior as well as that of the person they have a conflict with. Jerks always see themselves as the victim of circumstances beyond their control.

He also had a falling out with a friend/business partner and to this day I've never heard any real details about it. One time he said, "Other people may have a different story about what happened because they've heard it from him, so keep that in mind." Oh, the classic response – "You'll hear that I was at fault, it's not true."

—CF, 35, Vermont, abused 5 years

His employment is as a contractor, anything from 6 months to two years. The job he was in when I met him he was fired from after a month by some "f'ing whore" who told him "heads will roll" to which he responded "your f'ing head will roll." His previous job he was fired from because he was on a dating website during work time. When he tried to gain employment after that he struggled to get a resume, but none of this was his fault.

—Anonymous

Blaming the Victim

Ironically, Jerks can be extremely unforgiving of others they see as not like themselves, even though they let themselves off the hook all the time. While he may passionately defend behavior that is similar to his own ("I bet he didn't rape her, she's just lying to get hold of his money"), the real victims of life often get no sympathy at all. Poor people are poor because they're lazy. Kids act out because they haven't been spanked enough. Women get beat up because they're too stupid and keep picking losers. Black people need to quit whining about slavery and take advantage of all the great things this country has to offer. And so on. The main characteristic to look for, whether they are attacking or defending a particular behavior, is the sense of blame – there is one person who is being hoodwinked or taken advantage of and it's not his/her fault, or there is someone taking unfair advantage of a person or "the system." A Jerk is always looking for a victim and an aggressor, and often the "aggressor" is the person with the least power to defend him/herself from blame.

Avoiding Unpleasant Tasks

Another characteristic of low responsibility is the avoidance of unpleasant tasks. A Jerk usually feels he has special rights and shouldn't have to do things that he doesn't like. So he leaves his laundry around, or leaves the dishes for you, or doesn't fill up the gas tank, or doesn't pay his mom back for loans as he agreed. When forced to handle the messes they leave behind, Jerks will generally complain bitterly and try to make others feel guilty for making them do it. Or they'll act like they're doing you a big favor by "helping out," when they were actually largely or completely responsible for creating the problem. Procrastination can be frequent, as can broken promises, which are often not recalled or claimed never to have been made (you must have "misunderstood" again). As always, procrastination or avoidance of unpleasant jobs doesn't in and of itself mean you have a Jerk on your hands (I can be a serious procrastinator at times!). But it is an indication of low responsibility, and if it is very frequent or occurs in combination with other red flags, you should consider it a bad sign.

Financial Irresponsibility and Gambling

For some Jerks, their sense of entitlement includes the right to spend money they don't have and not pay it back. As a result, Jerks are often big borrowers. Their credit cards are over the limit, they owe their buddies money, they rob from Peter to pay Paul. And a Jerky partner will often ask you for loans as well. They'll be very sweet when asking, but if you say no, the pressure will mount, and it may even get nasty. Listen for the suggestion that you somehow are responsible for the consequences if you don't loan him the money. A responsible person knows that it's not your fault that he is in debt.

He gave me a hard time about not co-signing a car after we were only together for like 3 or 4 months. I kept fighting it and saying no. He cursed me out, told me that I was a bad girlfriend, that I don't love him, etc. I finally went against my gut and agreed because he's a good guy, we live together, why should I prevent him from getting a car when he needs one? Thought I was a bad girlfriend, but he was the Jerk forcing me to do something I was not comfortable doing. Lo and behold, he did a hit and run, destroying the car, his drug addiction prevented us from making the extremely high payments, 'cause he needed a really nice car, of course, and now I am like $30,000 in debt.

–SA

You should always get a good idea of the financial situation of your partner. If he owes a lot of money, find out what he owes it for. If he took out a business loan, did he ever create the business? How does he plan to pay it back? On the other hand, he may be taking out loans to pay for luxury items he can't afford (including that lovely, expensive ring he bought you on your second date!). Or he may be a gambler, or spend a lot of money on drinking or drugs. Whatever the reason, look for signs that he has taken out a reasonable sum of money and has a logical plan to pay it back. If he's speculating on some miracle happening, or doesn't have a plan at all, watch out! This guy is going to ruin YOUR credit and leave you with the bills. Financial responsibility level is one of the easiest areas for you to check out.

He told me he took care of the electric bill.… Summer in the south, pregnant and with no power and 95 or higher heat wasn't easy…he said he took care of the rent…he bought a van and we left a step ahead of eviction…

–KC

Another comment on gambling: many Jerks gamble. Why? Because you can make money without having to work, and if you believe the world owes you a living, you may think you deserve to hit it big and retire early. Naturally, you have to distinguish this from normal gambling for fun, which many people enjoy. But this kind of gambling is obsessive. There are fantasies and plans for how the money will be spent, or there are special "systems" that will assure he will win. He will be anticipating with assurance that he will win, regardless of the odds, and he will get very upset when it doesn't pan out. And most alarmingly, he may be planning to pay back his other debts with his gambling winnings. Anyone who gambles as a source of income is either not very bright or has a very low sense of responsibility. Gambling is not a career!

In general, any attempt to have other people be responsible for what happens to him is a bad sign. Not all irresponsible people are Jerks, but pretty much all Jerks are irresponsible. Lies, avoidance, and wishing things were different are not adult ways of managing the world. Someone who thinks like that is sure to be a nightmare as a partner.

> Early in the relationship, I asked questions on why his marriage failed. He told me that it was her fault, she was a bitch, her family got in the way, etc. I asked him why he didn't get the chance to see his kids, again her fault, then it was the ex girlfriend's fault.... When he suddenly quit his job, it was his boss's fault, his co-worker's fault. When we got into fights, it was my fault, I was over dramatic, I was a bitch, I didn't let him do what he wanted, I started the argument.
>
> —Anonymous

SOME SIMPLE TESTS FOR IRRESPONSIBLE BEHAVIOR

1) Listen to his response when he makes a mistake or is disrespectful or otherwise upsets someone. He may be able to publicly act as if he is sorry, but when he lets his hair down later on, listen to how he responds to conflict. See if he ever admits that he is at fault. Does he constantly blame others? Does he repeatedly come up with excuses as to why he could not succeed? Does he ever seem to re-evaluate his own behavior and make a plan to handle it better next time? Does his plan ever involve anything other than being more aggressive and intimidating in the future? A person who can't be wrong will never learn anything from his mistakes, including any he makes toward you. Pretty soon, you will be the scapegoat for anything that isn't going his way.

2) If you are noticing some stories that don't seem quite right, check them out. For instance, if he says he had to meet with his brother and that's why he missed your date, call his brother and ask how their visit was. If you find there was no visit, ask your partner to explain himself. See if he admits he was lying or comes up with a new story. See if the new story sounds as fishy as the old one. A true Jerk will have a hard time admitting that he lied to you, and will either get upset with YOU for confronting him, or create a new lie to cover his tracks. This kind of behavior is not something you want to mess around with. Liars make awful partners, especially when they can't admit they lie.

3) Do you find you have "misunderstood" him repeatedly, or that you often "didn't remember correctly" what happened? Do you start checking yourself to see if you could possibly have been wrong when you know you were right? If so, STOP! Start writing down what you and he agreed to and have a copy handy when he accuses you of a poor memory. Challenge him when he's blaming you for a misunderstanding and see how he handles it. When a Jerk is busted for lying or manipulating, you will see either a new outburst of "explanations" (none of which are his fault) or you will be attacked for "distrusting" him so much that you had to write it down. Either way, you've got trouble on your hands.

Alternatively, if he seems to have a hard time remembering his commitments, have him write it down, or write it down and have him sign it. If he really just has a bad memory, he'll be willing to go along with this experiment. If he avoids being "pinned down" to a commitment, or gets upset with you for trying to get a commitment, he's probably going to have a high Jerk quotient in other areas as well.

4) Does he often portray himself as the victim in situations where he actually has control? Does he complain about his ex-partners abusing him? If he has lost a job or been passed over for promotion, is it all someone else's fault? Does he blame political or economic problems on immigrants or the Arabs or some force outside of this country? Most importantly, does he blame YOU when he is upset about something that happened between you? Even if this blame is subtle or implied, be very wary of this. If there is a conflict between you, he should be making efforts to examine how he might have contributed to the situation. If it's always your fault, you may be certain you are dealing with a Jerk of the first order.

5) If you think you have a heavy procrastinator on your hands, make some concrete agreements with him to do something he doesn't like to do. For instance, if he doesn't like working in the garden, or cleaning the house, ask him to help you with one of these things, and set a time and date to do it together. Don't make it up – it should be something you need done, but schedule an actual time and see if he doesn't come up with an excuse. Or better yet, find something he's complaining about at his house and offer to help him with it, and press him to set a date and time. The key is scheduling the event and seeing if he tries to back out. If this happens all the time, it's a bad sign. It is true that some people are severe procrastinators and are otherwise responsible adults, but if you see this combined with some of the other signs, beware!

6) Look at his work history. Has he been fired often? Quit jobs for no apparent reason or because of conflicts with peers or bosses? Remained unemployed for long periods of time? As stated above, work history is an easy way to get a view of how someone handles conflict. If he has a hard time with it at work, you can bet he'll have an even harder time at home.

7) Ask about his finances. How does he handle money? Does he plan for the future? Does he spend more than he earns? Does he have big debts? Does he fantasize about some "big break" that's going to somehow solve his financial problems? We all dream occasionally about winning the lottery or getting on *Who Wants to Be a Millionaire*, but most of us understand not to plan around these unlikely events. A responsible person has an understanding about how income and spending relate. Not everyone plans for his/her retirement, but when expenses exceed income, a responsible person makes adjustments. A financial Jerk blames others, takes out loans, and guilt trips those who won't bail him out. No matter how charming and romantic and sweet and sexy he may be, this point by itself should be enough to convince you that the loving thing to do is break it off and tell him to come back when he's solvent. And if he is secretive or lies about money, you have double trouble on your hands.

8) Resist any attempts to merge finances early in a relationship. Don't pay his bills, don't loan him money (or let him loan you money, either), and by all means, don't open a joint account with someone unless you are committed for the long term. And as we said in Chapter 5, you want to avoid any attempt to manipulate, encourage or force you into an early commitment. If you are appropriately resisting a merging of finances, and he is in any way upset about this, it's a pretty good indication he's a Jerk and is trying to make you feel guilty about setting your own boundaries and rules. Don't give in to this kind of pressure, and watch how he reacts. If somehow you're supposed to feel bad because he's in debt and you won't help him, or because you don't "trust him" enough to put your own hard-earned money into a joint account, he's a very high risk to abuse you in other ways.

A lack of responsibility is one of the surest signs that you will have trouble later on in a relationship. Set high standards early and expect them to be met. Don't make or allow excuses for missed appointments, misunderstood communication, or poorly handled conflicts. If you expect mature, adult behavior from your partner, either he'll respect you and measure up, or you'll know that you are dealing with an immature, childish, self-centered person whose charm is a cover for his lack of responsible behavior. And if someone consistently gets upset with you for asking him to take responsibility for his own behavior, he is not a person you want to have in your life for the long term.

CHAPTER 7

Dependency/Clingy Behavior

THERE IS ANOTHER STYLE OF JERKINESS THAT WE HAVE ONLY TOUCHED on lightly so far: the passive Jerk.

Most people associate abusiveness, especially in men, with the common "macho" characteristics that men are taught to emulate: tough, unemotional, willing to handle conflicts with force or even violence, and an "in your face" attitude that says "I'm in control." But there are many abusive Jerks who look very different from this stereotypical picture.

These Jerks often appear quite emotional, sharing feelings and being very "sensitive." They may be into art and music, long walks, and romantic candlelight dinners. They may hate football, cry at movies, and think that being gay is just a normal part of being human. They may present as pro-woman, even as a feminist.

But what they have in common is their ability to convey a sense of emotional dependency on their partner. They want you to feel needed and they use this feeling to control and manipulate you, just as ruthlessly as their more aggressive brethren.

There are, of course, many Jerks who will combine this set of tactics with more aggressive approaches. And there are people who are clingy and dependent who aren't Jerks. But as you will see, screening for dependency is an important tool in your Jerk Radar toolkit. It can be one of the more subtle and vicious Jerk-laid traps that can be very hard to escape.

"Only You Can Help Me"

This is where the "Beauty and the Beast" myth comes into play. You, by your magical beauty, love and all-around wonderfulness, can solve any problem he has and make him feel good merely by being near and sharing your love. A huge number of romantic movies emphasize this theme of a loving woman helping a troubled or even nasty and unpleasant man realize how he can become a better person. Many, many women enter into relationships believing that "he'll change" under her gentle teachings. But in reality, this kind of change almost never happens. The Jerk is simply using this myth to sucker you into doing things his way.

Here's how it works: your partner sets up a scenario where you feel like you are providing him with support he needs, and that he deeply appreciates and values your help. For instance, he may have recently escaped from what he terms an abusive relationship, or a "bitchy" partner, and is struggling with the emotional aftermath. He comes to you for help, and you are able to soothe him and help him "move on" from his traumatic experience. He may even still be married or living with the person in question but framing his dalliance with you as a path out.

In any case, you have saved him from his suffering. He is very appreciative and lets you know that he wouldn't have made it without you, that you help him keep going when he wants to give up, that you are the bright light in his otherwise dark and depressing existence. His story is compelling and you feel great about being the one who could help him. His gratitude seems sincere and he seems to love being in your company. You get kind of a rush from knowing that you are filling an important role in his life and have helped him feel better about himself.

And now he wants to be with you. A lot. All the time. He

NEEDS you. He can't make it without you. He has to call you about important questions. He needs to talk to you at work every day to make it through to the evening. If he goes a night without seeing you, he falls back into his old depressive habits. Nothing makes him feel good except for being with you.

> Within a month of meeting him he encountered an "accident" at the gym on the day of my best friend's hen party [US term is "bachelorette party"]. I was supposed to be maid of honour & host the party. I ended up spending the night with him instead of with my friend, as his doctor had apparently told him he couldn't be left alone in case he suffered from concussion. As those first few months went on I became his "rock" as he struggled to get access to see his son. I found a lawyer for him, took time off work to take him to the lawyer, held him as he cried, spent hours and hours listening to him. He needed me to be available to him 24/7 in case he was feeling down…and I was. It wasn't unusual for me to get several phone calls a day asking where I was, what time would I be home, then I'd get home to find him on the verge of tears, and waiting to relay his tales of woe to me.
>
> —Anonymous

> Before our first date, he reeled me in at work, by asking me to help him find an attorney to fight his ex wife over child custody…. I was sucked in to his "needing me to fight that horrible bitch who took my child." Since I have gotten away from him and gained some knowledge on this issue, I see how I allowed myself to be used for his needs. And how I was the perfect tool for him to do so. He could sit back and let me do his dirty work and I would feel so "needed" by him. Actually, the only thing

he needed was someone to manipulate…and when his
ex left him, I filled that void perfectly.

–BK

Here we see a twist on the isolation game we encountered in
Chapter 5. Rather than using the romantic "love story" approach
to explain why you need to be together all the time, instead, his
need for comfort and love is so great that only you can provide the
necessary relief. To go out by yourself would be to let him suffer
needlessly.

This subtle guilt trip is combined with what can be a very powerful feeling of competence and worth in knowing that you are
the ONLY ONE who can help, and that you have turned his life
around just by being your wonderful self. This feeling provides the
same kind of intensity as the romantic charmer does when he "falls
in love" with you within days of your meeting, as we talked about
above. And as we already know, a Jerk wants to create maximum
intensity, because it makes isolation very easy to accomplish. This
is a VERY seductive approach and is easy to fall for, particularly if
you (like many people, including me) get a lot of your feeling of
value from reducing the suffering of others and helping to make the
world a better place.

In the beginning, even before we were committed and
boyfriend/girlfriend, he used to talk about his past a lot.
He would say that he never really had anyone who'd help
and understand him. He said how much he has suffered
because he didn't have a Dad when growing up; he said
how much he has suffered because he was bullied at
school; he said how much he has suffered because his
Mom never understood him or tried to be there for him.
He said he's far more sensitive than one would expect
from his tough guy looks.

…he began telling me how great it is that finally
someone wants to listen to him and help him. Soon, he

> began telling me how I was the only person who mat-
> tered to him, the only person who "gets" him, and who's
> able to take his mind off all the problems and hurts. Of
> course, this soon became one of the most important
> tools to isolate me from others. He called 3 times a day,
> "just to hear my voice and make sure I was OK and to find
> out about what I was doing." He told me he severely dis-
> liked being alone. If I said I have other plans, with family,
> friends, or alone, he became moody and clingy and
> would insinuate that by doing that, I was hurting him.
>
> –KK, Estonia, 30, 7-year abusive relationship

Not infrequently, the dependent strategy involves the Jerk
"helping" you in some way as well. You may both be in recovery
from "bad relationships" and he may have extended a helping hand
to you and genuinely assisted you in recovering or escaping from a
previous Jerk. This can create a very powerful bond, a sense of "you
and me against the world," which is very easy for a Jerk to exploit.
You have instant intimacy, a natural commitment that seems to
grow out of your mutual needs and not be artificially induced by
romantic charm in the way described above. In short, it seems completely genuine, and it is hard to believe that someone could enter
into this kind of exchange with ill intent.

> This blew my socks off. I had not had a "steady boy friend"
> before this, aged 20, and I was floored that he would
> want to spend all his spare time with me. G gave me the
> impression he couldn't do without me, and it did get to
> the stage I thought I couldn't do without him, either.
>
> –AS, 56, 13 years married, Australia

And in some sense, it may be genuine to begin with. This person
may actually feel they were treated badly in their previous relationship, and that you are a wonderful exception to the general rule
that most women are mean and heartless bitches. But remember

what we said about Jerks in Chapter 6: nothing is ever their fault. So he may genuinely feel "hard done by," and yet have actually been the one being abusive to his partner.

As always, I am not trying to suggest that two people recovering from bad relationships or difficult childhoods can't find love together and make a better life for each other. It happens all the time, and far be it from me to try and put a damper on such a beautiful result. But before you let yourself fall completely for this seemingly gentle, kind, and sad man, take a moment to check out a few things that might save you from a lot of trouble later on.

Where Is the Balance?

The first thing that distinguishes this kind of Jerky relationship from a genuine, mutually supportive one is the question of balance. A truly healthy relationship is one of give and take, one where roles are fluid and each partner at times gets to play the role of helper and of the one being helped. In an overly dependent relationship, this is generally not the case. While the Jerk may appear at first to be interested in hearing how you feel or what you need, this role is assumed temporarily for the purpose of getting you quickly and deeply engaged in the process of meeting his needs alone. The dependent Jerk will gradually, subtly, but insistently convey the message that his needs always come first. This will not appear to be because he is demanding or unreasonable, but because his suffering is so great that you simply have to put aside your own suffering for a moment to comfort him. These moments gradually stretch out into hours, then days and weeks and years, and sometimes partners wake up 20 years later and wonder what went wrong. But if you check for these signs early on, you may be able to prevent yourself from falling into this kind of trap.

So the first screening device for a dependent Jerk is to make sure that you take time to take care of yourself. Not to let him take care of you, but to take care of yourself. Because part of the dependency is to make you dependent on him for your own needs, in the early stages, he may be very solicitous about making you dinner, giving you a massage, asking caring questions about your abusive mother, and so forth. What he will NOT like is for you to be able to meet your needs without him there. So pick some things that you've always done to take care of yourself, and keep doing them, even if he wants to spend time with you right then. Play the piano, go for walks by yourself, paint a picture, play volleyball, read trashy novels or classy novels or hard-hitting non-fiction or whatever you prefer, but do it alone and see how he deals with it.

Common Jerky responses will be to come up with something you can do together (or asking you to think of something), to insist on doing the activity with you even when you've said you want to do it alone, to ask you to delay or reschedule the event because he needs you now, and if all else fails, to "support" your decision but at the same time act sad and sorry and depressed enough to make you feel guilty about it. This kind of diversion or guilt-tripping is very indicative of someone who wants you to think they can't get along without you.

> If I said I wanted to just be at home alone that night and not meet him, he'd act surprised. He said he didn't understand why I preferred being alone to hanging out with him. "If a couple is close to each other, they shouldn't need other people. I don't need other people. I only need you because I have fun with you, and you make me feel good and understand me, so why would I seek out other company? I don't understand...am I really not enough for you?" "If you go out tonight to visit your best friend, it would really hurt me. Don't you understand that I don't like to be alone at home without you? I'm so bored alone, and I start missing you the moment you walk out the door. We should go together, or you shouldn't go at all. Why do you always need to hurt me? I thought you were

different from all those other people who I never could trust. I thought I'd found the person who I could finally trust fully and who only wants to be with me. Obviously, I was mistaken."

–KK, 30, Estonia, 7-year abusive relationship

This use of "neediness" to control you is very subtle and easy to overlook – after all, he WANTS to do something that you want to do, he just wants to do it TOGETHER. What can be wrong with that? He must love you a lot to feel that bad when you're separated. Come on, it's just a walk, why not do it as a couple? He may even come up with some culturally supported explanations for why you shouldn't want to go for a walk alone. "Most couples spend more time together than we do." Or, "If you really loved me, you'd want to do everything together." Watch for ANY sentence starting with "If you really loved me…" Unless you're doing something pretty Jerky yourself, the odds are tremendous that this is an attempt to use guilt to control you into meeting the needs of your partner at your own expense.

I spoke with a woman one time when my wife and I were engaged, and I told her that we had separate apartments and slept separately more often than not. She said, "Wow, is something wrong with you guys? Are you having trouble?" When I explained that we both liked to have our own space sometimes, she was quite flabbergasted. Apparently, engaged people need to spend every minute together to convince her that they're serious. In truth, healthy relationships need space, but the dependent Jerk will not allow it. Taking time and space to care for your own needs is the best way there is to detect someone who expects you to always be there for them, no matter what your own needs may be.

Your own feelings can also be a strong indicator that you're being manipulated by a dependent Jerk. One feeling that I am very vulnerable to is the feeling of "being the hero." Your Jerky partner will note if you have this soft spot and will work it without mercy. If you often find that you are feeling the need to make the "noble sacrifice" for your partner, if he often compliments you on your selfless devotion or your willingness to put your integrity before your own needs, if you are getting most of your satisfaction in the relationship out of having helped out a fellow human being in trouble, you are probably in with a partner who is playing on your "hero button" a lot.

You may eventually start to feel a certain sense of resentment at times, which you will probably try to talk yourself out of. You may be feeling the need for a little space, and yet find yourself going along with his plans because he seemed so excited about it or was so insistent or looked so sad when you said what you were going to do. If you find yourself doing things or agreeing to things that you didn't really intend to do originally, take a look at how you got there. Were you just working together with your partner to come up with a mutually agreeable plan, or were you being worked BY your partner the minute you brought up something he didn't think of himself?

Moodiness

The next stage in the dependent Jerk's strategy is to introduce moodiness into the picture. Because he reports he is dealing with so many emotional challenges in his life, it may seem understand-able that he has bad days and is unaccountably upset or irritable. And maybe it is. But the way to tell the true Jerk from the person having a bad day is that normally, the person who feels bad does not think it's your personal job to make them feel better. Whereas your Jerky partner may believe that you have to do whatever he says to help him cope with his "bad mood." This may include a whole range of things, such as talking in a particular way, not bringing up certain topics, being quiet when you want to talk, not playing certain music he doesn't like, having to listen to music you don't like, cooking him meals, fetching him items, or even tolerating him being disrespectful to you, because "you know how I am when I get in these moods, you can't hold anything I say against me."

> He would say, particularly after a bout of abuse and I was asking him why he did it to me, for the umpteenth time, that he loved me so much and that I was his rock, his security, and that he couldn't live without me. And sometimes he used to cry as he was saying it. It was almost like a mother/child relationship…
>
> –TR, 25-year abusive relationship

This is how the dependency tactic really works: you get the message, very subtly at first, but stronger and stronger as the relationship develops, that your partner is sensitive and vulnerable and moody, and that your job is to ADAPT so that you don't "upset" him or her. The requests and demands become more and more unreasonable until one day you put your foot down. At this point, you get hurt looks and guilt trips and any kind of message that lets you know you have let him down. You are NOT the wonderful person he once thought you were. He believed you really CARED, but now he can see that you don't care at all about him. You are SELFISH!

This is reminiscent of "Beauty and the Beast" – remember when Beauty goes home to her family and doesn't come back on time, how the Beast is so depressed he's about to die of grief? Remember how Beauty had to return to him to make him feel OK, despite all he'd done to harm her and her family?

The accusation, however subtle, of you being "selfish" when you insist on meeting your own needs is the cardinal sign of the dependent Jerk. It is normal for people to have bad days, or to disagree with you about music, or to want to do one thing when you want to do another. But in a normal relationship, such conflicts are negotiated to a mutually agreeable conclusion. Whereas with a Jerk, their way is the only way to go, because they are just too weak or sensitive or vulnerable to handle it if you make your own decisions. Which leaves you in the crappy position of deciding to either go along with his plans, or not have an agreement at all.

"Trying" and Guilt-Tripping

Another typical strategy of the dependent Jerk is to say they will "try." When you confront them with some particular behavior that you find objectionable, they are often the soul of reasonableness. Let's say he was guilt-tripping you because you went for a walk when he wanted to snuggle with you. "You are right, I know that's a very bad habit I have. It all comes from my bad family, you know that I was sexually abused so I have a hard time with boundaries. I'll try to understand next time. You can go on a walk if you want to, I'll just try to deal with my feelings on my own."

Notice that even in agreeing to "try," your partner has made it clear that his "feelings" about you taking a walk will be something he needs to "deal with," suggesting that you are causing him to suffer. He also blames his feelings on something he can't control, namely his upbringing, so his suffering is certainly not HIS fault. He agrees to "try" to deal with his feelings on his own, but you already get the impression he'll make a bad job of it. So you are already primed to expect that your next walk will not happen without a certain degree of guilt feelings on your part.

Then when you actually DO go for the walk, this conversation seems to be totally forgotten! He's right back to, "Can't it wait until after breakfast? I'll make pancakes, your favorite!" If you remind him of your earlier talk and his agreement to "try," he may start off by saying, "This is a totally different situation," and explain why this time around, his need for you to stay is completely justified. If you insist, or eventually "convince" him that it is the very thing he was supposed to "try" to change, he will perhaps capitulate in a very hang-dog kind of way: "OK, you're right, I'm just being needy as usual. Go ahead, take your walk, don't worry about me, I'll be OK." This is commonly followed by either a big sigh or a long period of silence or some sniffles and tears, or a somewhat dramatized retreat to "take care of himself" (maybe with a door slam added for emphasis), suggesting that it will take some work for him to overcome the severe feelings of abandonment that your insensitive and selfish decision has caused.

Now it's completely possible that all these feelings are 100% genuine. That's not the problem. He can feel however he wants. The problem is that he is blaming YOU for causing his feelings, and making YOU responsible for making it all better! He's taken a very normal, human impulse, to take a walk alone around the neighborhood, and made it into an attack on his personal integrity and safety. Your behavior has taken on such intense meaning that your morning walk is all but ruined in wondering how he's coping with the blow.

This kind of emotional abuse is one of the hardest things to detect in the early stages of a relationship, because it fits so well with the cultural myths and expectations we talked about in Chapter 2. But by report of victims who eventually escape, it is often more damaging than the more obvious manifestations of domestic abuse, such as yelling, threats or even violence. It is harder because it works by making you feel responsible for the other person's experience, and makes you feel like they are the victim of your selfishness or cruelty. Most people will go far out of their way not to be thought of as mean or selfish, and these Jerks use that impulse to pressure you to go further and further from what you know to be true, to the point that you may eventually begin to question whether you aren't the one who is abusing him. But it all starts with the simple premise that it's always your job to make him feel better.

> He had back problems and would make sure I baby him – get groceries, help him rub in some pain stuff on his back, and of course, it got worse when I started to make plans on my own. Or he would suddenly say he

spent all money for trips on the doctor, and we had to stay home. In the end he would follow me around in his car – because he "missed me and wasn't feeling good and needed me."

—Anonymous, 24, Germany, abused 8 months

SOME SIMPLE TECHNIQUES TO DETECT AND AVOID THE DEPENDENT ABUSER

1) As discussed in Chapter 5, it is always good to avoid quick involvement, no matter how well you seem to "connect." The dependent abuser will want to spend every minute together and will want you to "be there" for him whenever he "needs you." Make sure that you are not always immediately responsive to his needs and see how he handles it. If he breaks down or gets irritable or guilt-trips you or does anything to suggest that he has a right to command your attention when he needs it, you should be very suspicious of his motivations.

2) Check out his complaints about his awful childhood or his "bitchy" prior partners. See if you can meet the people he complains of and decide how you feel about them. The fact that they are mean and nasty doesn't mean he isn't just as bad, but if he says they're awful but you find them kind and reasonable (in a non-manipulative way), you may want to start questioning his story.

3) Be doubly careful if you are also getting out of a bad relationship. This kind of abuser often actively looks for someone who is emotionally vulnerable because it's easier to form a quick bond with someone who has "suffered as much as I have." If you find the discussion frequently turning to how badly you both were treated and how lucky you were to have found each other, step back a minute and ask if you are being roped in. Relationships "on the rebound" have a bad reputation for a very good reason – they rarely work out well, and the timing makes you highly vulnerable to manipulation and abuse.

4) Check out your partner's support system. Who does he go to other than you when he needs help and a listening ear? Who could he get a hug from if he needed it besides you? What activities does he do to help himself when he's feeling bad? Has he ever considered therapy or other kinds of supports? Has he been seeing a therapist for 10 years but is still functioning poorly? Does he depend on prescription drugs or illegal drugs or alcohol to make himself feel better, but take no other kind of action (diet, exercise, community involvement, hobbies, career change, etc.) that would make the situation less onerous? Does he blame others for his feelings and experiences as discussed in the last chapter? Are his bad feelings largely the result of irresponsible decisions he has made in the past, such as getting himself fired from a job or getting into debt through gambling? You are looking for signs that he has a mature attitude, multiple coping strategies and a good range of supports available so he doesn't collapse with anxiety or grief when you go to the store without him. You don't want to be his sole emotional (or financial) support!

5) Make sure you always take time away from any partner to meet your own needs. This is the very best early screening tool for abuse through dependency. Watch specifically for any reactions to your choice to handle your emotions and needs on your own. If you find that other things always "come up" when you're about to go off on your own, if you find yourself feeling guilty for doing things that you like to do because he doesn't get to do them with you, if you ever hear that "if you loved him" you would do what he wanted, your Jerk Radar should be buzzing a loud warning signal. You have a right to do your own thing and take care of yourself. Anyone that wants to be with you all the time is going to be difficult to manage down the road, no matter how much fun they are today.

6) Overall, check the "balance factor" in your relationship. Make sure there is both give and take from both of you. If you find yourself giving in a lot and even mildly resenting it, if you find yourself doing less of what you like and more of what he likes to do, if you find that you get a lot of emotional resistance whenever you want to make your own decisions, take a hard look at what is going on. Healthy relationships thrive on trust and agreements that are mutually beneficial. The relationship should enhance both of your lives. If you end up feeling like his life is being enhanced at your expense, you may have hooked up with a dependent Jerk.

7) Watch out for guilt trips! These are the bread and butter of the dependent Jerk strategy. Accusations, no matter how subtle, of selfishness or neglect, are an indication of the kind of emotional self-centeredness that is the core of all Jerky behavior. Do an honest check and see if you are really being selfish, but odds are good that, unless you are habitually self-centered, you are just trying to meet your own needs in a way that doesn't meet his. Any attempt to make you feel guilty for doing normal things like making yourself a sandwich or practicing the guitar or listening to music you like at a reasonable volume should be met with a very assertive response.

8) Monitor any agreements you make with him and see if he is really "trying" or just saying he will to get you to stop bugging him. A truly considerate person will find the fact that they're annoying you sufficient information to change their behavior in noticeable ways. Trying should lead to observable improvements; otherwise, it's just a smokescreen for more emotional abuse.

9) Never accept his "mood" as a reason you need to walk on eggshells. You didn't create his mood and you aren't responsible for fixing it. You can listen empathetically for a reasonable period, and offer to make some suggestions if he's open to it, but just hearing him whine about how bad things are, or worse, allowing him to behave badly because you're worried you'll upset him, just leads to further abuse. Confront any "moodiness" right off by making it clear that you expect him to be respectful to you, no matter what his mood. If he can't handle that, give him the boot. As soon as you have to change your behavior in order to keep him from being upset, he's got you in a bind you may never escape.

Remember "Beauty and the Beast." You are not responsible for making his life work for him. He creates his own emotions and experiences, no matter how flattering it may be to believe that you can make his life better. We can't change other people, and are better off not trying, and instead focusing on making our own lives the best they can be. If you and a partner can make better lives together than either of you can alone, that is one of the greatest joys life has to offer. But it can't come at the expense of your own integrity. Be who you are and do what you love, and don't expect the two of you to share everything.

And if he is too emotionally fragile to handle you being an independent human being, get him a referral to a good therapist and say goodbye. You're better off without him.

CHAPTER 8

Attitude Towards Women

THIS IS A VERY LARGE AND IMPORTANT AREA TO EXPLORE WITH ANY partner. In a sense, this gets to the core of what distinguishes a Jerk from someone who is working to develop a healthy relationship. A Jerk is someone who believes they deserve to be served, bowed down to, or otherwise treated as if they are superior to their partner. This may not be apparent to you at first, especially when it's just the two of you together. But eventually you will see that this person's attitude is simple: Men are more important and women should do as they are expected. Which means HE is more important and YOU should do as he expects you to.

The Awful Ex

One of the earliest signs of this may be how he talks about other women, especially about former partners. It is not unusual for a Jerk to have several ex-partners, or even a large number, whom they will describe in very negative terms. Naturally, there are female Jerks out there in significant numbers, and it's possible that your partner will have run across more than one. But listen to how they describe their former partner's behavior. A person who has escaped from a Jerk will usually experience some level of confusion about their prior relationship. They may be frustrated or bitter about what happened, but they will also have a tendency to search their own hearts to see what they might have done differently to make things work.

A Jerk, on the other hand, will blame the entire failure of the relationship on their partner. They tend to use very negative and hostile terms to describe their partners, such as "crazy," "bitch," "slut," or similar insults. They will speak in general terms about them, saying things like "she never...," "she always...," or call her lazy, stupid, fat, ugly, or other such put-downs.

> My partner let me know early on what he thought about his exes. He described them as drunken, out-of-control, violent, needy, clingy, psycho bitches. I believed everything he said about them until he said the same thing about me. I was a sucker for his lies. I had been so abused by men, that I thought he went through the same abuse by women.
>
> —Anonymous

> Ah. Exes. Apparently all of his exes except one were abusive. They abused him, were psychos, bitches, whores, you name it. All the things I soon became. He told me sob stories about things they supposedly had done to him. But of course, he never touched them even when they were hitting him. He spoke very badly of his exes. I believed everything he said.
>
> —JD

"You Are So Different From HER!"

It is not unusual for a Jerk in the romantic, charming phase to make flattering comparisons between you and former partners: "You aren't a crazy feminist like my ex." Or, "Thank God you know how to work for a living, unlike that lazy pig I used to go out with." The insults may not be that obvious right at first, maybe more like, "She wasn't a traditional woman like you," or "she didn't pull her own weight like you do." But it is common that you will be favorably compared to an ex or to women in general as a means of making you look superior. If you listen carefully to these comments, you will hear a subtle message behind the words: "I don't like feminists, and if you want to keep me happy, you'll make sure to prove you aren't one." Or "I need you to make money or I won't find you acceptable."

Comments like these can be used to make you feel good, like you are better than the average woman, or that you are going to somehow help him heal from his past sufferings. That's part of why the charming or dependent Jerk will use them. At the same time, they help establish the most important point in the abuser's attitude toward relationships: as the man, he will decide what is acceptable behavior for you.

> In his case ALL of his ex-girlfriends were "bitches, cunts, fat," etc.... women clearly were everything negative to him, and he did treat me first as if I was the magical exception.
>
> **–Anonymous, 24, Germany, abused 8 months**

If you hear this kind of statement, it's not too hard to check out the intent, as long as you're not too worried about offending a Jerk's sensibilities. A pointed question can give you a pretty quick idea of what he means by these comments. Something like this: "So it sounds like you don't like feminists very much. Tell me about that." Or, "Why does it matter so much to you that your partner has a job?" These questions should not be hostile, but should be asked in an interested way – you are just trying to find out more about him, to understand where he's coming from. A normal person would be willing to tell you more about his values, or may go into an explanation of what happened to him that led him to these conclusions, and you will find out a little more about who he is that will help you decide if the two of you are compatible. But a Jerk will likely react in a different way.

Two things you will want to watch for. First, the Jerk may begin to expound on why all feminists are bad, or how women who work are putting men out of a job or are out to unman their mates, all of which shows an attitude of control and a need to feel superior to women. He may also add some stories about his crazy ex and the insane things she used to say and do that prove what a bad person she is. This is easy to interpret – he is putting her down to you, and you can bet that sooner or later, he'll be telling some other woman similar things about you.

Second, he may get defensive about the comment and either back off from it ("I didn't say that" or "That's not what I meant") or suggest directly or indirectly that you should not have asked the question ("What exactly do you mean by THAT?" or "Gee, you don't have to get so touchy!"). He may also simply ignore your question and change the topic. This is harder to read, and you may have to test it more than once. What you are looking for is an avoidance of answering the question. You also want to notice any sign that he is upset or bothered by the question itself. Either behavior suggests that he's worried about sharing what he really thinks and maybe has something to hide. The thing he most likely is hiding is the fact that he thinks he's more important than you could ever be.

As always, this by itself could just be an aspect of his personality – maybe he grew up around this kind of talk and needs some gentle or not-so-gentle education about what you will put up with. But combine this with any other sign and you may have trouble ahead. Put-downs or blaming of the ex are particularly bad signs that should never be allowed to go forward unchallenged.

Even if he doesn't trash the ex, there are plenty of other indications of a negative attitude toward women that can be very revealing. There are many behaviors that are commonly accepted and even laughed about, but are really indicators that your partner thinks he's more important than you are.

Stereotypes and "Jokes"

Starting with the obvious, any jokes or comments that put down women should be a red flag. Abusers often rely on sex role stereotypes to maintain their sense of control and superiority, and frequently test you out with these "jokes" and comments to see how much you'll tolerate. It should be a no-brainer that any partner who hates women is eventually going to hate you.

Some common beliefs amongst male Jerks include:

- A man should be smarter or more accomplished than his female partner.

- Men should earn money, women should stay home with the kids.

- Women shouldn't have to work, men should take care of them financially – you will insult him if you insist on working.

- If a man earns the money, it's his money and he gets to decide how to spend it (even if you have joint accounts, etc.).

- Worse yet, he may believe that he should control all the finances, even if you earn the money.

- Women make bad bosses, leaders, politicians, etc.

- Women who are bosses must have slept their way up the ladder.

- Women are moody or difficult due to "hormone problems."

- Cleaning house is women's work.

- Taking care of children is women's work.

- Women cook and clean up, men eat the food.

- A man who "helps out" with children, cooking or cleaning is a great guy, even if you still do 90% of the labor.

- Women should serve men dinner, beer, etc.

- Men should always drive, because women are bad drivers, or have a poor sense of direction.

- Female partners or dates should be ready to "put out" sexually if the man is interested.

- Married women can't say "no" to sex.

- Women who don't "put out" after several dates are "cock teases."

- Women say "no" to sex because they want to be pushed – women like sexually aggressive men; they say "no" but mean "yes."

- It is OK to speak of women in patronizing ways, such as calling coworkers "honey" or "sweetie" or referring to grown women as "girls" or "chicks" or "babes."

- Men should be dominant in relationships.

My ex had really strict and really inflexible ideas about what men and women should do. Cooking, doing laundry and dishes, cleaning and interior design (like sewing drapes and pillow cases and generally beautifying the place up) were chores that only a woman must do.... "It's the woman's job to do those things and to do them well, no matter if she works or not." "This is

> something that should come naturally to you if you're a real woman, you should have talent in these areas and you must enjoy doing those things, any woman would!" We both worked full time at equally demanding jobs but he always said that all the stuff a woman should do is solely my job.
>
> —KK, 30, Estonia, 7-year abusive relationship

> He's a hunter/fisherman and acts like it's such an amazing feat if a woman does those things. He's fond of saying, "It's just natural...men do (this or that) and women do (this or that) better."
>
> —CF, 35, Vermont, married 5 years

Now it is even possible that you may believe some of these things yourself, if said a little less negatively. That's perfectly OK for you. But the belief in male superiority over women is the core of many an abuser's value system that allows them to be Jerks and feel OK about it. This kind of statement or belief, especially if combined with other "red flags," is usually an indicator of serious Jerkish tendencies.

Men with these attitudes often engage in "humor" that is really a put-down to a woman or women in general. This can be as mild as "dumb blonde" jokes (which always end up being about blonde women), and can go so far as to include "jokes" about rape or assault on women. When challenged about these things, the response will generally be, "Oh, it's just a joke," or "Where's your sense of humor?"

> He constantly made jokes about how women were inferior to men and really thought that women weren't equals especially because they aren't capable of being physically strong like him in his field of work. For example, although I was going to school to be a teacher,

it was never going to be as hard of work as the physical labor that he did.

—SA

Even though my ex is overweight, he has an attitude towards women who are overweight. Many times in the grocery store parking lot we'd have to wait for pedestrians to pass. He had terrible things to say about the overweight females who passed by. He'd say they are fat pig-bitches. Or he would mimic a truck noise backing up…BEEP…BEEP…BEEP.

—Anonymous

These "jokes" may also extend to other minority or low-status groups that are commonly the target of put-downs in our society. Jokes or negative general comments about blacks, "Polacks," Italians, Mexicans, gays, lesbians, immigrants, Muslims, feminists or any group of people that are the subject of common biases should be considered a bad sign.

This kind of "humor" reflects two things: first, it suggests a tendency to generalize about others, rather than recognizing the wide range of individuals belonging to any group. This is bad for you, because it suggests both a lack of empathy and a willingness to use common prejudices to justify irrational hostility toward someone he doesn't even know. Second, it suggests a need for your partner to find someone to feel superior to. You can bet that if he needs to feel superior, sooner or later he'll need to feel superior to you. While a certain amount of insensitive "humor" is not uncommon in otherwise decent people, it is definitely a red flag. When it is combined with other indications of anti-woman biases, it is a good sign that trouble is ahead.

Negative comments about women or any "other" group as you mentioned were frequent. And, of course jokes in very bad taste. He had a few favorite jokes he'd like

> to tell at parties and I always cringed when he started
> it. I told him how offensive I thought they were and that
> would just make him laugh harder or accuse me of being
> uptight with no sense of humor. It bothered me more so
> that he really seemed to think these were the funniest
> jokes ever when really they were so lame as far as jokes
> go and really just immature.
>
> −CF, 35, Vermont, married 5 years

This is even more significant if your partner also makes serious and unapologetic negative remarks about other groups. Male Jerks are commonly very down on feminists or assertive or powerful women in general, calling them "dykes," "bitches," "castrating," or saying that all they need is a good man to screw them. These anti-woman sentiments should set off alarm bells in any partner. Not only is he making aggressive and negative generalizations about people he doesn't even know, he is making it clear to you that you'd better not be a "feminist," which most likely means any woman who stands up for her rights. You don't have to subscribe to radical feminist doctrines to be swept up in this generalization – it's really a protest against women being regarded as having the same rights as men. You can do the math and see where this kind of thinking about male-female relations is likely to lead.

Generally bigoted remarks about blacks, gays, Muslims, etc., including the use of insulting names to refer to them, are also very strong signs of a bully who needs to dominate others to feel secure. This also includes bigoted beliefs such as the idea that "Mexicans" or other immigrants are taking over the country, or that anti-bias laws have made employers biased against white people. Aggressive putdowns of gay people in particular tend to go along with a hatred of women, because to be "gay" for such a man is to be "feminine," and for him, to be feminine is to be worthless. He may be treating you like a queen right now, but sooner or later, you are going to be put into one of the "bad groups" of people and will then be fair game for his punishing comments and behavior.

I remember we once watched the news and there was a clip there about a Gay Pride event. He started talking about how "those perverts should all be locked up or deported to some other country which wants them." I was shocked and told him that he's insane, they haven't done anything wrong. That made him really angry. He went on and on about how gay people are perverted and when children see them, they'll be corrupted too, and because they're corrupting us "normal" people, they should be locked up so they wouldn't bother anyone. He did make racist jokes too and when I would tell him not to make them because they were not funny and were in fact discriminatory, he'd just make them even more often on purpose and tell me that I just didn't have a good sense of humor.

−KK, 30, Estonia, 7-year abusive relationship

Treats Women Badly

General treatment of women other than you can be an indicator as well. We've already mentioned that put-downs of former partners are a very bad sign. Listen also to see if he talks very negatively about his mother, sister, aunts, movie stars, coworkers, or any woman he sees on the street. I am not talking about making specific and reasonable observations, like "My mother is very rude – she interrupts all the time and doesn't listen" or "My sister always seemed to resent that I got better grades than her." I'm talking about trashing someone: "Doris is a bitch – she's probably slept with the boss to get promoted," or "Look at that slut – her boobs are hanging out. She's probably looking to be screwed," or "My sister is so stupid – she can't even clean house without a guide book." I'm not talking about specific complaints; I'm talking about insulting remarks and generalized put-downs that say "I am better than she is."

He had a very negative attitude towards women in his family. He said his sister is a slut and his mother a bitch.

> I would never go out with a man who says such things
> again – even if they make comments like that jokingly.
>
> —Anonymous, 24, Germany, abused 8 months

Also watch his interactions with other women. Does he consider them to be less important than men? Does he ignore women in social gatherings? Does he expect them (or you!) to fetch him things, clean up after him, give him the TV controller, or otherwise defer to his orders? Does he make negative remarks or "jokes" about women in front of them? How does he respond if his mom or sister challenges him, or does not follow his direction? In particular, watch how he treats his family, or how men treat women at one of his family's gatherings. If it's considered normal for women to be servants, or for women to stand by quietly while they are insulted, it is very likely that he will expect you to accept a similar role when you are a family together.

> The last day I spent with my ex I awoke to him ranting
> & raving about work, his boss was a woman and he was
> shouting about her incompetency, he rounded it off by
> telling me "I hate women anyway!" His mum came to visit
> a while back, she's old and frail, in her eighties, I guess.
> She feels the cold as she's not from this country. She was
> tired & wanted to go to sleep, so he ushered me out of
> the living room, gave her one thin fleece throw and no
> pillows, and left her to sleep on the floor!
>
> —Anonymous

Goddess or Whore?

Another variation of this that may be harder to catch is that abusers may put certain women on a pedestal, describing them in such glowing terms that no real person could live up to this standard. He may do this with his mother, and be very upset with you finding the slightest fault with her. It may also be his sister or aunt or some other female figure. But the tendency of many Jerks is to divide the world into two categories of women: goddesses and whores. This kind of black-and-white thinking about women is bound to lead to trouble. A man with such beliefs will undoubtedly put you in the "goddess" category to start with, and much of the charming behavior, as well as some of the beliefs about how you "shouldn't have to work" and how the man takes care of the woman, come from this idealized view of you as goddess. Problem is, no one can be a goddess forever, and sooner or later, he will decide you aren't measuring up to his unattainable ideal. And since there are only goddesses and whores, and you no longer fit the "goddess" ideal, you know what that makes you.

Of course, some idealization is completely normal, both towards mothers and sisters and of course, toward you early in a dating relationship. It's OK if he thinks his mother or sister is a wonderful person and thinks them a bit better than humanity in general. And it's definitely OK if he views you through rose-colored glasses – it's normal and healthy to believe your partner is better than most, otherwise why would you be together? What you would be looking for is a particular sensitivity to ANY weaknesses or flaws in his idealized woman, especially if it is combined with some of the other attitudes we've described earlier in this chapter. Any tendency to divide women into the perfect and the horrible is a big red flag.

Admiring Bullies

One last point to check is his attitude toward men, especially men in authority. A man who is a great admirer of other dominating and bullying men is not someone you want to be around. Look at who he idealizes – does he think that Napoleon, Alexander the Great, or even people like Hitler or Stalin are the height of male accomplishment? Does he identify with aggressive, dominant or bullying males in movies or TV shows? Does he like to listen to music or watch music videos where men are dominant and women are "hos" or "bitches?" Does he tend to put down any men who are sensitive or kind as "wimps" or "sissies" or "fags?" If he hears a news story about rape or domestic abuse, especially involving a sports star or other celebrity, does he consistently believe the woman is lying or exaggerating, or made it up to get someone's money or to get her name in the paper? Does he speak highly of a father or brother or friend whom you believe to be kind of a Jerk?

A tendency to admire or make excuses for the powerful and blame the victim for being weak is something you want to watch out for. Especially when combined with other items in this section, it probably indicates a belief that he should be allowed to dominate you because you are weaker than he is, and that he will be justified in punishing you should you step out of line. This is a central belief of a significant majority of Jerks and something you want to stay far away from.

SOME WAYS YOU CAN CHECK FOR ANTI-WOMAN TENDENCIES IN YOUR POTENTIAL PARTNERS

1) Ask him about his former partners. Listen for put-downs and generalized remarks about them. If he says, "She was such a bitch!" ask him for specifics as to what she did that was so mean. Don't accept "she always" or "she never" – get him to describe a particular incident or two that were problems for him. If he can't or won't provide specifics, he's probably making it up, or covering up what he did to cause it.

If he does talk, listen to his description – does he talk about what he might have done to improve the situation? Does he appear confused or exasperated, or just hostile toward her? Does his anger seem out of proportion to the situation? Does he seem to be asserting "rights" that he shouldn't have, like expecting her to read his mind or clean up after him or lend him money when he's spent all of his own? These incidents will tell you a lot about what his values and priorities are, and what he expects from a partner. If you can easily see yourself doing the same things that this "bitch" of a partner did, you probably ought to make this date your last.

2) Does he compare you favorably to his prior partners? If so, ask him to tell you what specifically is so different about you two. Listen carefully to his answers. Listen for tendencies to trash the other partner, to put you on a pedestal, or to state unreasonable standards that the partner should not have been expected to meet. Ask him to tell you what was good about his former partner – "You were in love once – what made you fall in love with her?" An inability to give a reasonable answer to this question should be a big red flag. This would suggest that he probably doesn't really get to know his partners. He instead creates perfect fantasy images of them that no one could live up to. Which means sooner or later, you will "disappoint" him, and the consequences may be worse than you can imagine.

3) If he gives you specifics about his partner(s) that he hated, ask him why these things are so bad. If she "never cleaned up," ask him what he feels she should have done. Find out how he feels about sharing cleaning responsibilities. Ask how he thinks men and women should split up household chores. If he finds these questions upsetting, or if he is clear that he expects you to do all the work and him to get all the benefits, you might want to consider if you really want that kind of arrangement.

Or if he says she spent too much money, ask what she spent it on and how much she had and whether he "gave" her money for shopping and so forth. Jerks often feel they should be in charge of dealing out the money, sometimes even when their partner actually earned it. He may also be upset when his partner can't stretch the insufficient money he gives her to make ends meet. This kind of monetary control is a sure sign of trouble.

Whatever he was upset about, ask for details about why it was a problem for him, and what kind of constraints the partner was operating under. If you listen, you'll gain an understanding of what he expects of a partner and how he reacts when his expectations are not met. And if he gets upset with you for asking, you know you have trouble on your hands.

4) Religious beliefs can also be a good way to check on this area. If he has a religion, ask him what his faith community believes about roles of men and women. Ask him how closely he subscribes to these beliefs. What you are looking for is more than just what his view of these roles is. It is actually more important how flexible he is about areas where you might disagree with his values. He can believe that women should stay home and take care of the children if he wants to, but does he expect YOU to be that way, just because he believes it himself? How will he deal with it if you want to work and he wants you to stay home? Does he think he has the final say?

While he may not be completely honest with you about any of these questions, his reactions and statements could give you some insight into his attitudes toward women and partners.

5) Check into his values regarding men and women. This is a very normal topic of conversation in any relationship and can easily be pursued without anyone taking offense. If he does take offense at the topic, you're really in big trouble! But if not, ask him to share with you his views on male-female roles in a relationship. As we talked about in Chapter 3, remember not to tell him what you think first, or he'll start telling you what he thinks you want to hear. Catch him at a relaxed moment and ask him to talk about how he sees relations between the sexes. Watching the news or movies or TV shows can be really good times to bring this up casually, as many examples present themselves in our media.

If he's a normal guy, you will find out a lot of interesting information and be able to exchange views and hopefully come up with a greater degree of harmony on this important topic. If he's a Jerk, you will most likely discover how he views women as inferior to men. You can even try out a few probes into things that Jerks often believe. "Do you think women secretly like to be dominated?" Or: "What do you think of feminism – do you think we've gone too far?" Or: "Did you hear about [some famous person] who was charged with beating his wife? What do you think about that?" Keep these questions very open ended, so he doesn't have an idea what you think and can freely expound on his views. Listen for any indication that he feels women can sometimes deserve to be abused or need to be controlled for their own benefit, or that women are out to get men and make up abuse allegations to get back at them. Review the list of beliefs earlier in the chapter and see how many fit him. One or two may be OK, but if he's matching up on six or seven or more, he's a high risk to be Jerk material.

6) His sense of humor will be very revealing. Make careful note of what he regards as funny. How many "jokes" are about putting down or making fun of others, especially those who are powerless to defend themselves? Does he often laugh when others are hurt or humiliated? Does he think horror movies involving abuse and murder of women or powerless victims are amusing? See if you can hear him in a group of his buddies rather than just the two of you – it's much harder to hide your real personality in a group than in a one-to-one interaction. Movies, TV shows and news stories are also great places to see his "real self" slip out. Don't overlook these "lapses" – they can provide real insight into what your potential partner believes and values. Humor says a lot about who we really are, in a way that's hard to hide. This ought to be a part of every Jerk Radar screening.

7) See if he regards himself or his group as superior to others. Does he put down blacks, whites, aboriginal people, immigrants, Frenchmen, communists, liberals, conservatives, children, the elderly, the mentally handicapped – in short, does he spend a lot of his time figuring out who is lower in social status than he is? This reflects insecurity and a need to feel superior that will undoubtedly soon be applied to you.

8) Similarly, does he regard some people as worthy of hero worship? Does he look up to sports stars, movie stars, political or military figures? If so, ask him why he thinks they are worthy of his particular respect. Look carefully at who he thinks of as his heroes. Are they controlling, powerful, or abusive? Does he admire them for getting away with things or for overcoming the opposition? Does he have empathy for the oppressed, or does he identify with the people doing the oppressing? A lot of Jerks idolize people who are in power and use it to dominate others. While this in itself doesn't tell you who he is, if it happens in combination with other signs, it should be cause for serious concern.

9) In addition to his statements about women, watch how he treats other women, especially those in positions he considers inferior. This would include waitresses, receptionists, clerks, his secretary at work, janitors, or anybody he would consider "beneath" him in the social order. Also look at how he treats his mom, sister, grandma, or daughters. Many Jerks will act lovely toward you but will treat other women like trash.

I once worked with a guy who was always extremely respectful to me personally. We were peers in the workplace and I was a man, so he regarded me as his equal. But then I heard him talking about a woman I also worked with, who I felt was an incredibly hard worker and who always asked me for more to do to keep busy. He talked about how she wouldn't do as she was told and that she avoided work and should be brought under more control and authority of the supervisors. I was shocked! But I found out that he treated her like an inferior. While I always requested her help, and thanked her for what she did, he ordered her around and showed no appreciation for her contributions. I figured he got the results he deserved. But you never would have guessed he would treat anyone that way based on how he treated me. He clearly viewed women as inferior and treated them as such.

It is important to note that some Jerks will be perfectly charming with all women in whatever capacity. The absence of poor behavior doesn't mean he's OK, but if he does generally treat women badly, you can assume you will eventually be treated the same way.

10) You might also be aware of any signs that he's "hitting on" someone else. Of course, he'll deny it, but don't overlook it. Jerks who are very concerned with sexual conquests are almost always "keeping their options open." A certain amount of flirtation can be normal in any male-female interaction, but watch for those excessive charm indications that we talked about earlier. He may be lining up his next victim just in case you don't work out.

I actually know of a guy who e-mailed three or four women at once and told them all he loved them and wanted to date them exclusively. (He sent copies of the exact same e-mail to each of them!) He went through the responses and decided based on the response time and what was said which one he would pursue. He'd been with his partner for years but she was starting to set some limits, so he wanted to be ready with a substitute in case she bailed out on him.

You may not personally notice any flaws in his behavior toward you during the courting period. The questions above can help you see what he will really be like once the "honeymoon" is over. If you genuinely want to protect yourself from being involved with a Jerk, checking out his values is probably the surest way to do it. Even the smoothest operator will show a few chinks in his armor. His attitude toward women and those he considers "beneath" him may be the easiest way to see through the charm and find out who he really is.

CHAPTER 9

You Play by His Rules

I WAS NOT ALLOWED TO PHONE HIM, EVEN TO SAY I WAS GOING TO BE LATE. If I ever called, I was lectured long about how I was checking up on him. However, he could phone me every five minutes if he felt like it for any reason he wanted. When he phoned so often, I mistakenly thought it was love.

I was not allowed to say I'd like to come too, even to the vegetable market. I learned early, and for ten years did not ever say it. However, almost everywhere I went, he said, I'll come with you. Then, he'd lecture me about how we did everything together.

–TK, 59, Canada, abused 10 years

This one may not be obvious right at first, but it's a standard for any real Jerk. Whatever else may be true in these pages, a true Jerk always believes that there are different rules for him than for the rest of the world. He is special and is entitled to special treatment, and anyone who thinks differently is either stupid or dangerous.

Perhaps the most common belief among Jerks is the idea that they have the right to make up all the rules. A large part of this is expressed as a lack of respect for any limits or boundaries you may set up. While this can be extremely subtle, it's also often one of the first things that can be checked for, even when your Jerk-to-be is in the full-on charm phase.

Essentially, for most Jerks, you're not allowed to say "No" to anything they want. In the later phases of an abusive relationship, this belief may be enforced by violence, threats, or other forms of direct force. However, the early phases are much more likely to be characterized by a manipulative style, where boundaries may be verbally acknowledged but subtly and intentionally undermined, bit by bit, often without you even noticing it is happening. If you suddenly find yourself doing something you had no intention of doing, or putting up with something you thought you said you didn't want, you're probably being handled in this way.

Jan describes how Mark used to plan trips for her that he told her nothing about. He not only expected her to go along with it, he expected her to be excited about it, even when he planned a trip to a place he knew she would not like. But if she had ideas, he would always change them in some way. She proposed a camping trip to a nearby national park, telling him how she loved camping and hiking. He agreed to do this, but actually booked a motel nearby. They never hiked at all.

On one occasion, Larry and Annie were boating together, and Larry had asked Annie if she'd like to steer. She said she would, but not at "the Point" (where two very big rivers join together), because she knew there were strong side currents and she was afraid she couldn't handle it. When they approached the Point, Larry abruptly told her to take the wheel, because he was going below. It was clear to Annie that this was NOT by chance – he knew she didn't want him to do it and he chose to do exactly what she'd asked him not to do.

"Misunderstandings" Revisited

We talked some about how common "misunderstandings" are in Jerky relationships in Chapter 6. Misunderstandings really do occur in all relationships, no matter how careful or skilled you are in communicating. But they tend to occur in a kind of a random fashion – you will misunderstand your partner about as often as he misunderstands you. And usually, there are good reasons why the misunderstanding happened that make sense to you after you look back on it. For instance, you may have agreed to meet your partner at the Starbucks, and you thought it was the one on Fourth Avenue, but he meant the one on Seventh and thought you knew that was what he meant. You find out what happened, usually both people apologize or take some level of responsibility, and you plan for it not to happen again. Nobody is hurt or wrong, and life goes on.

But an abusive "misunderstanding" can be taken to another level. It is sometimes actually intentional, meant to establish control over you by making you doubt yourself. And somehow, whatever happens, it seems to be you that has to make the adjustments. Using the same example, the abusive person will tell you to meet him at the Fourth Avenue Starbucks, and then wait for you at the Seventh Avenue branch. After waiting an appropriate period of time, he'll call and say, "Where are you? I've been waiting here for 15 minutes!" Notice that already, YOU have made HIM wait – it's already being implied that you've done something wrong. Then you tell him you remember him saying it was the Fourth Avenue Starbucks. And he assures you that it was Seventh. You must have "misunderstood" him. And you are sure in your mind that he said Fourth, and you tell him that, but he assures you that you got it wrong, he said Seventh, but it's OK, he knows that you sometimes get things mixed up.

You are still sure that you are correct, but there's this nagging doubt now that maybe you got it wrong, maybe you aren't remembering correctly. After all, this could happen to anyone, we all "misremember" things (as George W. Bush once put it). Maybe it was you… But you will notice that at no time did he admit the possibility that HE might have "misremembered." He assured you that you were wrong. Bad sign – even if it was a "misunderstanding," he's not willing to be wrong. And even worse, there's a good chance he KNOWS he was wrong and did it to mess with your head.

> One of the key things I did not catch onto right away was this – he asked what I wanted, and then it was always his way. It was small things, such as "What would you like for dinner?" Then, once I answered, he'd say, "Well, we're having such and such (something else)." I'd always say, "Oh, that's fine too." It extended to where I wanted to travel, cycle, walk, shop etc. He always asked, but it was always his way. He just took over without further discussion.
>
> This is confusing. You get the message from the asking that he is interested in your wants, but it's just an act. So, if he asks and does not follow through, he's making all the rules and hiding it behind "manners."
>
> —TK, 59, Canada, abused 10 years

This kind of "crazy making" behavior is very common for abusers and is often seen long before anything more overt starts to come out. Again, it starts with the belief that he gets to make up the rules, and if he wants to be deceptive about what he said, it's all OK. Of course, if you ever actually told him the wrong location to meet, both you and he would easily agree that it was all your fault. And if you INTENTIONALLY told him the wrong place, he'd be all over you like white on rice! So he's allowed to play mind games with you, but you're definitely not.

If you are noticing that you're doubting yourself a lot after talking to him, that you are becoming unsure of things you were certain of before, if you find that you are frequently "misunderstanding" what he said or meant, or that he's frequently misunderstanding you, but either way, it's somehow your fault – odds are you are courting a Jerk.

> If we were going to have a takeaway, he'd ask what I'd want and I'd say Chinese, and he'd order an Indian…he'd ask what night I wanted to go out. I'd say Friday, and we'd go on Saturday. It was just endless…it was just another form of control, but wrapped in pretend thoughtfulness.
>
> —TR, 25-year abusive relationship

Emotional Manipulation

Another way to set the rules up without being obvious is through emotional manipulation. This can take many forms, but one of the most common ones is the guilt trip. In this case, the Jerk implies that you are somehow disappointing him by your decision and that only a mean and heartless person would ever deny him what he wants. This can be combined with pouting, the silent treatment, and some of those not-so-funny "jokes" we were talking about earlier. Suppose you were going to spend a night out with some girlfriends, as you always used to before you went out with this guy. His response might be, "Oh, honey, I thought we were going to spend the evening together!" (You have not made any such promise to him, but he may "remember" you saying that you would – this is a great place for him to suggest you may have "misunderstood" or "misremembered" again.) "I was going to take you to the movies, remember that one we wanted to see together." He has never told you this, and probably just thought of it minutes ago when he realized you were going out without him. If you ask him why he didn't tell you, "It was supposed to be a surprise." "Come on, you can see the girls any time – we always have such a great time together. I can't imagine spending the evening alone when I thought I'd be with you – you KNOW how you turn me on, baby. Just do this for me, you can tell them you'll see them next week."

This could sound like an innocent attempt of an infatuated lover to spend as much time as possible with the woman he loves. But it most likely is something more. Notice how flattery is mixed in with the emotional pressure to capitulate. Notice how you are somehow held responsible for "disappointing" him, even though he didn't include you in his plans. Notice how easy it would be for him to make all of this up on the spot if he needed to divert you from your plans.

Of course, it's possible that on a rare occasion, your partner may have had surprise plans and be disappointed that you aren't available, but a more normal response would be to express his disappointment and leave it to you to decide what you want to do without trying to sway you. And such "surprises" should be pretty rare. If you find that they are happening a lot, and that they just happen by chance to coincide with you wanting to do something yourself, you should be on the alert. More importantly, if you decide to stick to your plans, he ought to respect that decision, even if he is disappointed. Attempts to pressure you to change your mind once you've decided what you want to do are clearly abusive, and should be challenged as such. If he doesn't back down when confronted, you probably have a major Jerk in your life.

> It was OK for him to lie to me constantly about anything and everything but the one time that I did lie to him over something really, really trivial, it was held over my head for a very long time.
>
> —SA

Silent Treatment

The "silent treatment" is another game that an abuser can play to manipulate you. Suppose you want to make dinner and go to bed, but he wants to go out to a restaurant. You make it clear what you want, and he stops talking. He may throw a couple of hurt looks at you, but otherwise says nothing. You ask him what's wrong; he says, "Nothing." But he continues to act like he's hurt, saying nothing but displaying nonverbal signs of emotional distress. He keeps up like this until you start to get upset, at which point he says, "Well, I did want to go out, but you obviously don't want to, so I figured there was no way. I didn't want to pressure you, so I was just keeping quiet." Of course, he DID want to pressure you but didn't want to admit to it. In the end, you probably end up going out to keep him happy, and feel somehow that you've been had. This kind of emotional pressuring and game-playing can really get into your head.

> I worked hard all week and would often want to just relax on the weekends but we had to go and spend most of the weekend with his family. My family were sort of introverted, sedate, reserved, quiet; his was loud, extroverts; I felt uncomfortable around them because they were so different to my family and I was extremely shy. This made no difference. If I didn't do what he wanted he would sulk, make those not so funny jokes but ultimately make me feel like a big jerk.
>
> –AS, 56, Australia, 13 years married

Similarly, he may act seriously emotionally distressed about something, setting up the situation that you feel you can't leave him alone without seeming like a heartless jerk yourself. He may pull out that he was just remembering how his mother died 10 years ago this month, it's really getting to him. "But that's OK, if you want to go out with the girls, I'll be OK, I'll just go up to my room. You know I get these depressed spells… (Tears start to fall…) She was such a great woman…sniff, sniff…I just wish I didn't have to be alone tonight…"

Most of us really don't want to believe that someone could truly be that manipulative. We would try to comfort the person before we went, and the Jerk would make sure it didn't work, so we'd end up staying in to "help him," and maybe even feeling pretty good that we made the sacrifice for the important cause of helping a loved one. Little do we suspect that the loved one set this up for our benefit, and he feels a small sense of victory that we changed our plans for him.

Double Standards

If you are further along in the relationship and have committed to each other exclusively, or even if you haven't yet but he wants you to, you may notice common double standards around contact with the opposite sex. You may find that he flirts with other women, but it's completely unacceptable for you to even talk to another man. He may have female friends he visits with when you're not there, but you'd better not be meeting your male friend without him around, or he'll suspect you are cheating on him. He may make admiring or sexually suggestive comments about other women he sees, but get upset when you notice a guy is cute or has a nice butt.

Of course, you may have noticed that our society supports a high level of sexual double standards. For instance, a man who sleeps with a lot of women is a stud; a woman who sleeps with a lot of men is a slut. Women are sexualized in the media in ways that men are not (although there are increasing numbers of sexualized pictures and roles for men in recent years). This gives great cover for the Jerk to exercise his personal double standards in order to get more control over you and your behavior.

> He was allowed to flirt, go out with other women when out of town on trips, see his former girlfriend in private, have women on his knee at parties. I was not allowed to stand within two feet of another man. I went to a movie with a male friend once when he was wining and dining with his ex-wife and her family, and he was very angry that the first thing I did when he turned his back was go on a "date" with someone else. This old friend and I had NEVER been anything but friends. If another man even

looked at me, he got all chest puffy and angry. He went on vacations and to dinner with his ex-wife.

–TK, 59, Canada, abused 10 years

This is not something you should tolerate. Even though there are social double standards, you have a right to make your own decisions about whom you associate with. A Jerk will attempt to convince you that "people will talk" or that your behavior is inappropriate, even though he engages in the same or more extreme behavior all the time. He may even overtly explain how it's different for men and women, men can get away with certain things that make a woman look bad. Any kind of double standard like this should be challenged early and often, and if he has a hard time handling your "independence," it's time to start looking for a partner who respects your rights from the get-go.

This may even go so far as him going out with, kissing, making out with, or sleeping with another woman, and then somehow blaming you for it. You weren't "putting out" enough, you were too busy, too cold, had your period, whatever. Or else he "couldn't help himself," he "made a mistake," he "lost control" because "she was coming on to me." Ask yourself this: if you made the same "mistake," exactly how understanding would he be? If he would not tolerate this behavior in you, why should you not hold him to the same standard? If he's allowed to do things you are not, he's playing the "I make the rules" game with you, and you need to take action.

He expected sex whenever he wanted it but if I tried to initiate it, he'd flat out reject me but then later on would blame me for not initiating sex more often...

–SA

He was allowed to chase and go out with dozens of different women, whereas I was in trouble even for looking at another man. He could stay out late with no explanation as to where he was or what he'd been doing, but I would have to account for my every move on the rare occasions when I went out. He could be late for just about everything, but if he was waiting I had to be on time, or else. If he wanted to go shopping we had to spend as much time as he needed, but when I went then within minutes he would soon make his displeasure known about how long I was taking, and he would then sulk.

–TR, England, abused 25 years

As we talked about in Chapter 8, these double standards often are extended to areas like housework and cooking. Any assignment of differential roles where he gets to tell you what your job is should be a red flag. Any situation where he gets "extra credit" for doing things he'd have to do for himself if you weren't there should set off your radar. You're not the maid or the cook or the gardener or some servant who should be happy when the "master" throws you a bone. It's OK to have a division of labor, as long as it's an honest negotiation and agreement. If you want to divide the labor up along traditional lines, where he does the car, the lawn and the trash, and you do the dishes, the vacuuming and the floors, that's great. The question is not how the jobs get done, it's about how much of a say you have in the decision. If he makes the rules and you have to follow them, you are probably heading for trouble down the line.

Kitchen Control

I got a lot of stories from my Jerk survivors about kitchen standards. Not surprisingly, it seems to be very common that Jerky men assign kitchen duties to the woman. But what I didn't expect was that the Jerk would often present himself as an incredibly capable cook, take over in the kitchen, and assume the role of Master Chef. This role, of course, entitled him to give orders to his "prep cook" (i.e., you) to do whatever he wants. If you find your partner taking over in the kitchen and giving you orders on how you are to help him, take a moment and consider if he's doing this to establish control over you and put you in your proper place as "his woman."

He Controls the Children

If you have children, you may also see him making up rules for them, or for how you should be parenting them, even if they're not his biological children. He may discipline them harshly, or demand that you do so, or he may intentionally undermine your authority with the children by letting them do things that you have forbidden, or letting them off the hook for things you told them to do. This is especially true for blended families – he will want to be the rule-maker for ALL the children, but may even treat "his" children with special privileges or scapegoat "your" children and expect you to do the same.

> He had a daughter who was 6 years old also. She imme-diately bonded to me and my girls and became one of us. He HATED this. She was HIS child and he hated that she loved us. He started acting like my girls were out of control and he set all kinds of impossible rules for my daughters, but not for his. It was hell for my girls, and his.
>
> I remember that he used to go to work and we would have a ball, playing in the pool, playing dress up, doing all kinds of fun girl stuff. Then, about an hour before he came home, we would scramble to get the house spot-less and remove all evidence of any "fun" times. We never spoke about what we were doing, but we knew. One day, his daughter made the mistake of telling me she loved me in front of him…
>
> –BK

Bottom line: abuse is about control, and Jerks like to control you by making up rules and expecting you to follow them. It may be subtle, but this is something that will start to show itself fairly early in the relationship, as soon as he feels he has sufficient control to start making you dance to his tune.

SOME QUICK TESTS TO SEE IF HE'S PLAYING "I MAKE THE RULES" WITH YOU

1) If you are noticing a pattern of misunderstandings, in addition to what was recommended in Chapter 6, you can specifically start asking him if it's possible he might have misunderstood you or remembered incorrectly. Start doing this every time such a "misunderstanding" arises and watch to see if he can admit he might have it wrong. Normal people will acknowledge that possibility; Jerks generally won't.

2) Try telling him you know you remember correctly and want him to acknowledge that. See if he can. It will be like pulling teeth for the true Jerk to admit to the possibility, especially if he intentionally set it up so you'd disagree. Of course, any hostility toward you asserting your reality is a sure sign he will escalate if you push him. You don't want to spend your time with someone who can't allow you to have your own reality. He will literally drive you crazy. And probably enjoy doing so.

3) If he is trying to guilt-trip you or use the "silent treatment," pretend you don't notice. Force him to be explicit in his concerns, and if he won't, just go forward and do what you need to do, and pretend his behavior doesn't even register. Since we know the purpose of these techniques is to have an effect, if it doesn't seem to affect you, he'll change tactics. If you see him suddenly move from grief-stricken to angry, or from ill to just fine in a short time frame, you know you're being manipulated. Of course, you have to ask yourself if playing this kind of game is part of what you want in a relationship, but the first step is seeing it for what it is – a game.

4) Continue your relationships with people of the same gender even if he seems to object. If he has a problem with it, ask him if you have given him any reason not to trust you. If he starts talking about his "issues," just bring it back to the question: have you given him reason not to trust you? If this doesn't bring him around, you should quickly make other plans for your future.

5) Set clear boundaries in the sexual arena and stick to them firmly. Let him know right away that you do not appreciate being pressured to do anything, and he'd better not even think about it. If he can't handle that, dump him immediately. He's going to be big trouble.

6) Also make it clear that you will not clean up after him from day one. It's one thing if he's coming over as a guest for a couple of hours, but if he is a regular visitor to your house, he should clean up after himself – wash his own dishes, pick up his socks, throw away his trash, recycle his own beer cans. Not that you can't do things for each other, like you make a nice dinner for him and clean up because it's his birthday, but don't let him start thinking that you're his servant. If he ever tries to order you around, even gently or playfully (and especially in the kitchen!), make sure he knows that you're not willing to play that role. If he has a hard time with that, send him on his way. You are not a servant!

7) Pursuit is not love! I really shouldn't have to say this, after Chapter 2, but if you've told someone to go away and stop bothering you, and he doesn't, this is an absolute deal breaker. He is disrespecting your boundaries and rewriting the rules to say that he gets to pursue you even if you say "no." This has huge implications, especially when it comes to sexual behavior (see Chapter 12). So regardless of the Mariachi Band or the rose petals on your apartment walkway, see this behavior for what it is: STALKING! If you have said no, he needs to respect that, absolutely and completely. Anyone who doesn't is going to be very bad news.

8) In general, the important thing is for you to decide for yourself what is right and wrong, and what you want in your life. Anyone who wants to tell you how to think, what to believe, who to hang out with, how to manage your own children, or how to feel, is someone you don't want as a friend or lover under any circumstances.

The tricky part is when they take an indirect approach and leave you wondering what is really happening. The best answer I know of is to take any situation where you feel something is being implied and either ignore it or get it clearly out on the table. If you think he's guilt-tripping you, say so: "You want me to feel guilty because I'm going out with my friends." "You are saying you don't mind but you're still trying to get me not to go." "You are telling me that my recollection is wrong." This kind of blunt, direct labeling of behavior makes it impossible for him to continue any covert attack. If he's being genuine, he'll apologize for giving you that impression and clear up what he really means. If he starts attacking you or denying what he's doing, saying you're paranoid or otherwise putting you down, it's because you're hitting him where he lives. That kind of reaction should send you running for the exit.

Mind games are part of every Jerk's repertoire. Don't fall for them. If you call a spade a spade and are not afraid of his disapproval, most abusive Jerks will run the other way after a date or two. You have a right to honest negotiations regarding rules and agreements, and the ability to negotiate honestly is the hallmark of a healthy relationship. Don't be afraid to test him out thoroughly on this point, and dump him if he fails. I hope you'll agree with me that it's better to be alone than with someone who is willing to make up rules for you just to prove he's more powerful than you are, or drive you crazy for his personal amusement.

CHAPTER 10

History of Abuse

A FTER THEY'D BEEN TOGETHER A FEW WEEKS, MARK DISCLOSED TO JAN that he'd been arrested in the past. He said he'd been convicted of selling drugs to teenagers. He explained that he needed to do this to help finance his college education. When she pointed out that he was hurting unsuspecting youth in order to make a profit, rather than agreeing and stating that he regretted his actions, his only response was, "I was in jail for a while. I paid my dues."

It might seem like this one should be obvious, but a lot of people ignore or minimize a history of Jerky behavior that seems to conflict with the romantic gentleman they are seeing now. Abuse history is the single best indicator of future abuse and it should be considered in every relationship as critical information before you ever get serious with a new person.

There's a saying in social work: "The best predictor of future behavior is past behavior." This is not to say that people can't change – many people make big changes in their lives and seem very different than they were years before. But there are a couple of conditions that almost always have to exist for a person to change.

First, they have to recognize that there is an issue or condition that needs to be changed. They have to acknowledge that there is a problem which will require them to behave differently or it is VERY likely that they will continue in whatever behavior pattern they have adopted. Consider the drug addict. S/he may have experienced severe consequences of drug abuse: losing jobs, car wrecks, having his/her license suspended, failing in school, losing relationships, being broke and in debt – and yet s/he may continue to completely deny the connection between substance abuse and his/her troubles. Such a person will not stop using until they recognize that substance abuse is the problem, rather than mean bosses, evil police officers, or unreasonable partners.

Second, even if a person recognizes the problem, s/he has to be motivated in order to change his/her behavior patterns. It is not enough for the addict to say, "Yeah, I know drugs are ruining my life. I really need to stop." Changing ingrained habits is HARD WORK, and they have to really, really want to do it. And almost always, it will require working with someone else, and being vulnerable and taking personal risks, whether it's a treatment program, AA/NA meetings, or working with Uncle Fred, who successfully kicked the habit a few years back. Signs of a person changing a drug habit might include seeking counseling, reading books on recovery, using "recovery language," staying away from people with whom s/he used, making more responsible decisions, paying others back for damage they did, and so forth. These are hard things to do and require a real commitment. In the absence of this kind of commitment, almost all people will continue to behave in ways they learned to behave early in their lives.

So if a person has been a Jerk in the past, it's likely he will continue to be a Jerk with you, even if his current behavior suggests otherwise. And it is almost certain that a Jerky partner has left some signs along the trail behind that he may not be the wonderful guy he wants you to believe he is. Gathering a good, accurate history of any partner is a critical component of your Jerk Radar.

Criminal History

The most obvious and hard-to-hide manifestation of Jerkiness is a criminal history. Now some of you will object and say, "Lots of people get in trouble when they are young and grow out of it." This is true. But you still want to know what it was they did and how they supposedly grew out of it. Most people, especially those who have really "grown out of it," will tell you if they have a criminal history and talk about how and why it happened.

So you should ask in the course of conversation if he ever got in trouble with the law. See what he says about it. A person who has worked through issues will explain how he came to believe that his criminal behavior was OK and how he justified it to himself, as well as how he later came to decide that he was wrong. As stated above, the key considerations in hearing these stories are 1) does the person recognize that he had the problem, and 2) how motivated was he to change his own behavior?

If your new partner has shared this kind of history, listen to how he tells the story. Did someone else "make him" commit the crime? Were the police somehow to blame? Were the courts unreasonable – did they convict him when they should have let him off? Did the DA act "unfairly" by not offering him a plea bargain? Or even worse, does he say he admitted to the crime so he wouldn't serve jail time but he was actually innocent? All of these statements would indicate he has failed to take responsibility for committing the crime that got him arrested or convicted.

> The story J gave me was the first time the guy robbed the convenience store and J was in the get-away car, he was parked blocks away and said he didn't know what the guy was up to. Then he said this same guy robbed another convenience store and again J was in his get-away car parked blocks away. This time he got caught and spent 18 months in jail. He said he was 18. He is a convicted felon.
>
> His explanation? He kinda laughed while he cupped his head in his hand and didn't look at me. He laughingly said he didn't know what the guy was doing.
>
> —Anonymous

What you are hoping for is something more along the lines of, "I was a dumb kid and I went along because I was trying to impress my so-called friends." Or, "Once I got arrested, I realized what an idiot I had been." Or, "I was lucky to get off with probation – I could have served three years in jail for what I did." All of these statements suggest a person who is responsible for his actions and recognizes that he was arrested because he made a mistake, not because someone else was trying to do him in.

Of course, there is the odd situation where a person was arrested for no reason – "Driving While Black" or other biased behavior by police or the courts. But be suspicious of such stories at the beginning and look for signs that indicate this is a strange exception that the victim is baffled or outraged about. Watch out for anyone who is constantly badmouthing police, the courts, or "the system" for victimizing them. Odds are great that he is minimizing his own contribution to the problem. If EVERYBODY is prejudiced against him and EVERY arrest is caused by bias and unprofessional behavior, you should be very wary that this person is more likely a con man than a victim.

If your potential partner claims not to have a criminal history and you suspect he might, get a criminal history check done. Arrests, charges and convictions as well as restraining orders and no contact orders are generally a matter of public record, and for a few bucks, you can do a little safety screening. Some women who have escaped abuse will not go out with someone without checking their criminal records first, no matter how wonderful they seem. If you have any doubt, check it out. And if they have a criminal history they haven't shared with you, especially if it involves interpersonal crime, it's time to look for a new potential partner. He's already covering up and lying before you've even gotten warmed up – it's going to get ugly later on!

The nature of the past charges is also very important. There's a big difference between being busted for marijuana possession or an "open container" in a car, as compared to being convicted of assault, child molestation, rape or domestic abuse. Any history of interpersonal crimes, no matter how long ago and no matter how well explained, is serious cause for concern. This is especially true for restraining orders, domestic violence assaults, sexual assaults, and child or pet abuse charges.

> I met my ex husband when I was seventeen and had just left school. He was twenty-two and had just left prison for "glassing" someone in the face. He was also due in court for smashing up a wine bar, and had been banned from driving for twelve months for drunk driving. I thought he had been treated harshly, I used to cry whenever he spoke about being locked up, felt so sorry for him. I never realised until after my divorce eighteen years later that he may have been abusive. I was seeing a therapist, she labelled him as cruel, the thought had never occurred to me, he was just how he was, I was used to it, everyone loved him…
>
> —CH

Restraining Orders

I haven't known an abuser yet who told me, "Well, I beat up my wife because I was being an asshole and that's why she has a restraining order against me." It could happen, but I've never met one yet who did in over 20 years as a social worker and counselor. Generally speaking, the Jerk will portray himself as the victim: "You know how women can just go down and say to the courts, 'He beat me,' and then you are screwed." Or "She was the one who was violent, I was just defending myself." Or "We were both violent – she upset me and I hit her back." While it is true that there are a very small percentage of cases where people swear out false restraining orders, the majority have been shown by studies to be true and real. In fact, things are usually at a very bad place when someone feels the need to go to that extreme, and usually the behaviors listed in the order are a small fraction of the abuse that really happened.

> He also mentioned once that a girl had accused him of raping her many years ago, but that she was a drunk and a druggy and that nobody believed her. I didn't believe it either because he was never remotely sexually violent with me.
>
> –EG

So a restraining order is a big red flag. While it is an outside possibility that your partner may be telling the truth and his partner was the Jerk in the relationship, the odds are substantial that the person who is being restrained did something to earn it.

This kind of charge merits very thorough investigation. You will want to see a copy of the order and read what was alleged by the person writing the petition. You should also ask to talk to someone else who knows about what happened, whether the prosecutor or a witness or the stated victim herself. If there is a conviction that went along with a restraining order, even if he has a great explanation, the odds are overwhelming that you are with a serious abuser. And if he has had more than one restraining order, you can safely assume they were totally legit and that you may eventually be filing one yourself if you don't stay clear of him.

Another very serious red flag is an order keeping him from seeing his children. Again, it is common for Jerky partners to come up with an explanation that blames others and makes them look like the victim. But these days, the courts, at least in the US and the UK, are remarkably strong about maintaining contact between parents, even when there is abuse in the relationship. A parent who is legally restrained from seeing his/her children has almost always done something particularly bad, or has repeatedly refused to comply with reasonable court orders and restrictions. There are exceptions, but these are generally very rare, and the courts are much more likely to err in the direction of allowing contact with people they should not. So a legal no-contact order with children is a very, very bad sign, especially if your partner takes no responsibility for having anything to do with causing it.

> Everything that I discovered or found out about was ALWAYS the other person's fault. The Orders of Protection from his ex-wives were all trumped up charges in order to keep him from seeing his daughter. System was against him, he pleaded guilty just to avoid a big mess and to save his ex some embarrassment, etc. He got in a fight at work (he is 54 years old for goodness sake! with a 24 year old)…but it was the other guy's fault, although he got suspended for it, etc, etc. etc.
>
> –BK

Has He Really Changed?

It is quite possible that your partner will fully admit to any of these crimes or actions, and even take some level of accountability – "I was young and stupid" or "That was during my 'drunk and disorderly' phase but I've grown a lot since then." And this is quite possibly true. Which brings us to part two of our test – is there any indication of motivation to change?

If he is now "different," ask him to explain how he got to where he is now. What beliefs did he have then that are different? What kind of process did he go through to realize that he had to change, and to discipline himself to make those changes? What exactly HAS changed? Does he still drink? If so, why should you think his "drunk and disorderly" phase has come to an end? Does he hang out with different people now? How does he decide who he hangs out with to avoid the troubles of the past?

Also, did he get help for his problem? Go to treatment? Counseling? AA/NA groups? Did he talk to his mom/dad, siblings, a special friend? Did he move to another city, take up some different habits, join some positive groups? What did he actually DO to make a difference?

Behavior change is very hard. You will want to see some signs of genuine thought and effort that went into the changes he claims to have made. Some Jerks are quite ready to admit to past violence or criminal actions. They may even tell you on purpose to test out your tolerance for a violent past. The key is to ask what kind of things he did to change the pattern. If he can't tell you specifically, he probably hasn't changed much, if at all.

> I recall him telling me about how he "forced" himself upon another girl (i.e. raped her) – he justified it as being because she had led him on and teased so much that he no longer could control himself.
>
> I also recall a story about him and his friends kicking rabbits about the park (yes, live rabbits) that were kept as pet in a pets corner in a community park. I remember crying at the story and being revulsed and disgusted. As soon as I reacted this way he backed off and said it was his friends that did it and not him.
>
> –SG

Secretiveness

A couple other things to watch out for. First, if he doesn't want to share details or explanations of his criminal past, he is most likely hiding even more bad stuff he didn't get caught for. And if he gets upset at you for asking, you know you are in big trouble and should get a cab home as soon as you can. A person who has really changed his ways will usually be interested in talking about the process. Even if he may be embarrassed about it, he won't be particularly defensive about the truth. A Jerk won't want to share, or will choose selectively what to share in a way that makes you feel bad to doubt him.

> My husband was very secretive about his past relation-ships and gave me very little information. He said they

were in the past and had no relevance to our relationship. I think this would be a red flag for me now. It
seemed weird to me at the time. He was put in prison
for GBH [Grievous Bodily Harm – a British designation for
a level of assault] when he was in his twenties but said
this was due to a bad phase he was in at that time and
he was through that. He said when he reached his forties
he had worked through a lot of these issues. He was a
bully at school. He was bullied himself when he started
secondary and then he turned bully to get everyone
back for what they did to him. He blamed his wife for the
failure of his marriage but eventually I saw she had really
done nothing wrong.

–FS

"Don't Hold My Past Against Me"

Which leads to the second point: If he is challenging you in any
way to "not hold his past against him," you will want to watch out
as well. Sometimes the Jerk is setting you up to teach you that you
had better not hold him accountable for his past actions. He will
share his past but will expect you to exonerate him or to agree that
it's all in the past and should be forgotten about. This is not a good
sign at all. He is asking you to let him off the hook about things in
his past, most likely because he will be doing things in the future
he wants you to let him off for as well.

I only had what he told me to go on. I knew his ex had
been to see a lawyer because of his behaviour after they
split up, I saw the letters, but he swore it was her not him
who'd been abusive. He was really upset at the accusations she made towards him. She wouldn't allow him
near her home because of his violent threats, which I did
witness, so I ended up collecting their son on his behalf.

He used to threaten to chop her f***ing head off & bury her in the ground covered with concrete.

–CH

Talk to the Ex

Unfortunately, a criminal record only covers a very small range of Jerky behavior. A huge percentage of domestic assaults go unreported by the victim. Of those that are reported, many end up with no arrests or no charges filed. But more significantly, domestic assault is generally only the tip of a very large iceberg of Jerky behavior which led up to the big blowup that involved the police. Things can be incredibly awful and dangerous for a partner but never get to the level of police involvement.

Which is why it's a great idea to talk to past partners. Especially if you've seen any other red flags talked about in this book, see if you can talk to some ex-girlfriends, even ones he just went out with for a short while. Have a friendly chat with them about their experience with your potential partner. Did he seem honest to them? Was he responsible? Did he come on really strong at the beginning and press them for quick involvement? Did he show irrational jealousy or paranoia about her talking to other men? Did he keep tabs on her or control her friendships/family relationships in any way? Did he gamble, drink, or use drugs? Was he unfaithful? Ask her any of the questions that we've talked about in this book, and compare her answers to his.

> One should always listen to the ex-wife...
>
> One of the most important things I remember was his telling me that he punched his first (or was that his second) wife in the face when he discovered she was cheating on him. He told the story in such a way that I felt sorry for him. When I look back on it, I don't know how he managed to manipulate my thinking so that I

thought he was justified and was a sympathetic figure in it all. When I met her later on at a memorial service, she said to me "You must be a really nice person because he is really a Jerk." Somewhere in there, my brain was messed with. They blind you to the truth.

–TK, 59, Canada, abused 10 years before escaping

Of course, I do understand that an ex can be bitter and blow things out of proportion sometimes, so you have to evaluate if this person is relating facts or just acting out her feelings. Ask for specifics. "He's a bastard!" may sound bad on the surface, but find out what he DID that made him a bastard and you'll be in better shape to put her comments in perspective. That being said, a relationship that ended with that kind of bitterness is not necessarily a very good sign, either. So don't dismiss comments made in anger or resentment – just ask for the details of actual events, and see how they fit with the picture your charming man is putting across.

Don't forget to ask how he was in the beginning of the relationship as well. If he started out as charming, sweet and kind and suddenly seemed to change into someone else, he's almost certainly a major Jerk who is playing you. Look also for confusion and self-doubt on the part of the ex: "I don't know why he changed. I wondered what I had done wrong. He seemed so nice initially – I guess he must have some problems. I tried to help but nothing seemed to work." Any statements like this indicate that the person you are talking to was trying to make things work, and her partner was playing games with her head.

Be sure to ask directly if he was ever violent or threatening to her. Some people are ashamed of what happened to them or are afraid they will be judged, so they don't share this spontaneously. But most people will tell you if you ask them, especially if you are clear you're looking for information and help in evaluating him as a partner. A lot of abuse victims have a fantasy about telling the "new girlfriend" to look out, so she may be very happy to share the details once she realizes you really want to know and won't be

upset with her for sharing. If there are ANY incidents of physical or sexual abuse, police calls, threats, weapon use, or other indications of overt violence, RUN LIKE HELL from this guy. I don't care how nice he seems or how he explains it away – this kind of information is almost a 100% guarantee of abusive behavior that you will soon be experiencing.

Another really great check is to ask her how the relationship ended. Did they come to a mutual conclusion that it was over? Did he dump her for another woman without warning? If she was the one who left, did he accept her decision? Did he pursue her afterward with multiple texts, e-mails or phone calls? Did he try to charm or guilt-trip her into "giving him another chance?" Did he threaten violence or suicide? Did she take him back multiple times against her better judgment because she felt bad for him or he promised to change?

A Jerk is generally more interested in controlling the situation than changing his behavior, but can be very persistent and convincing that things will be different in the future. A cycle of separation and getting back together, especially if threats or manipulation are involved, will again be an almost certain sign that this person is not interested in relationships except to meet his own needs. A mature person will be hurt and sad if a relationship is over, but after a short negotiation period, will come to accept that things are the way they are. He may even maintain friendly relations with the ex. A Jerk, on the other hand, will only allow things to end on his terms. So you see either a sudden and complete abandonment, usually for a new "perfect woman" who will now meet all his needs, or an obsessive clinging, with alternating pleading, charming, and threatening behavior, as an effort to pull the victim back into the Jerk's circle of control. A particularly bad sign is if the ex did everything he could to get her to take him back, and then dumped her himself after she gave him another chance, as a punishment for her dumping him. That kind of vengeful behavior is something you don't ever want to experience.

Psychiatric Hospitalization (Sometimes)

A much softer sign, but still important to check, is whether he's ever been psychiatrically hospitalized. A lot of totally fine people end up in the psych ward for a while, so this is definitely not a deal breaker. But there are two big things you want to look for: was he in for threatening to hurt someone, or was he threatening to kill himself in the context of a relationship ending? The first is kind of obvious. The second is a remarkably common but misunderstood tactic where the abuser tries to get the victim to feel guilty for "causing" him to be suicidal when she tries to escape from his abuse.

If either of these things are true, you will want to talk it over with him, and check again for the indicators of responsibility I mentioned above – does he recognize that HE has a problem or blame "the system" for overreacting? And if he "has changed," what has he done to indicate that change is real, and how did he manage to accomplish it? There are some inspiring stories of recovery from even severe mental illness that will make you want to weep or applaud, but it doesn't happen without a lot of commitment, insight, and just plain hard work on the part of the person making the changes. Especially if the hospitalization was for violence or victimizing behavior, you will want to proceed with a great deal of caution.

> He said his father used to beat 7 bells outta him, and then he was sent to a reform school aged 12 run by the priests. There he was abused (I know he was truthful about that as I seen his compensation award papers). But he was jailed for attacking and nearly killing a man in a pub. He told me the guy came onto him and he freaked out because of his past abuse. So I bought it. But he was a manipulating, devious little s***, who [I later discovered] beat his wife.
>
> –IM

Reputation

Reputation in the community can also be a good indicator, although not as reliable, because some Jerks are known as upstanding citizens and seem like wonderful people until you are in a relationship with them. So a good reputation should not wipe out any concerns you have based on other sections of this book. But a reputation for violence, abuse, or self-centeredness is something you want to check for.

Friends and family frequently make off-hand comments about this person they know so well that can be quite informative. Watch for statements like, "He's a great guy, but he's got a bit of a temper." Or, "He sure goes through women fast." Or, "I never did get why anyone would go out with someone like him."

> NOBODY told me WHAT he did! Nobody told me that he had a temper, was a wife beater, had an order of protection...NOBODY. About ten people warned me that he was not good to get into a relationship with, but they never would tell me why.
>
> –BK

> [I had] repeated warnings from his friends and family about what a "s***head" liar, manipulator, user, narcissistic creep he was. But, he was not showing me that part of himself to me, and I did not heed any warnings. In fact, I defended him.
>
> –TK, 59, Canada, abused 10 years

Any of these comments should be followed up on immediately. "You said he has a temper – what did you mean by that? Can you give me a couple of examples?" Ask for very specific details of incidents that made this person think he had a temper, or was a bad risk for a relationship, or whatever it is they believe to be true. It is possible that one person may just have a bad relationship or have had a bad experience with this guy or be a Jerk him/herself, but if

multiple people say he has a temper, you can bet he has one, and odds are it's probably worse than they say. Similarly, ask friends and family about issues of substance abuse, criminal history, even what he was like as a child. If he's OK, you will learn some things that might enhance your relationship. And if he's not, you may learn some things that will help you realize early on that he's a bad risk.

> I learned that his father thought about warning me, but he didn't. I didn't really know him well back then and I really think I would have believed my husband more at the time anyway.
>
> –CF

You can also check with friends and relatives for information on prior relationships. Find out how he relates to women. If he has a reputation as a "Don Juan" or a womanizer, you will want to know this. If he has had ugly breakups or gone back and forth on separations with the same woman, these people will know about it. If he has a tendency to initially idealize a woman, and then later demonize her, these folks can tell you about it. And if you find that their stories don't add up with what he's telling you about himself, you will learn that he's being dishonest right up front. In particular, check for any stories of violent or abusive behavior from this guy, including manipulation, guilt trips, and dishonesty. Not everyone will be willing to share, but even one good source could save you from months or even years of confusion and suffering.

Of course, you should also ask him about these things directly. If he says he has a "bad temper," you should believe him! If he says he has "issues with women," don't be surprised if he has issues with you. If he says he has "anger issues," know that you are going to be the target of them. As I mentioned above, abusive Jerks will often raise these issues directly with you to see how you react. Don't reassure him that it's OK and you don't mind, or have faith he'll work things out!! Don't delude yourself into thinking you can "help him

with his issues." Instead, go right after the issue: "You said you have anger issues – what does that mean? What kind of things have you done? When do they happen and how often? What are you doing about these issues?" If he gets upset by you asking these questions, you can bet your next paycheck he's a Jerk trying to soften you up so you're not surprised when his temper "causes" him to do something you won't like. "What do you expect – you KNOW I have anger issues!"

Don't shy away from asking these direct and challenging questions. You may be worried that you will scare him off with this kind of behavior, but the only people who will be scared off are the ones you don't want to have anything to do with in the first place.

Firearms

One thing that often gets forgotten is to check for this person's attitude toward firearms and other weapons. There are folks who collect old swords or World War II rifles or who have a set of hunting rifles in a cabinet in the hallway. These are not necessarily anything to worry about. What you are looking for is an obsession with weapons – holding, shooting, talking about them a lot. A big, emotional attachment to weapons usually means a big, emotional attachment to power and control, and that's not something you want to be around. Especially if this person keeps loaded guns around unlocked, talks a whole lot about the right to bear arms, or plays with weapons or knives, you want to strike them off the dating list right away. If this person has ever assaulted someone with a weapon or threatened to, don't even bother looking any further – you don't want to be around them. The most dangerous abusers are often the ones who love weapons. Check with friends, family, and ex-partners about this one. Your life may depend on it.

His Attitude Toward the Powerless

Lastly, a person who is Jerky to others will likely be a Jerk to you as well. Look in particular at your partner's attitude toward people who are relatively powerless in society. He may be charming as heck to you but be disrespectful to his little brother, or his aging aunt, or his neighbor's dog. Abusive behavior toward children, the elderly, or pets is highly associated with abusive behavior toward a partner. If he shows disrespect toward those who are vulnerable, the odds are very good that once he has you in a vulnerable position, you will be next.

> When he told me he trained his dog by cracking a rubber hose across his nose, I should have known. I mean what moron does that? It is sadistic and potentially life-threatening for the dog.
>
> —TK, 59, Canada, abused 10 years

Don't make excuses for a person's past behavior or let him make excuses to you. Always expect your partner to take full responsibility for any bad behavior in the past and demonstrate to you why you should not expect this behavior to continue into the future. This can be one of the best screening tools in your arsenal. While it may seem socially "rude" to challenge a partner in this way, it is your own safety and sanity that is involved. Never be afraid to speak the truth and to expect him to do the same. Anyone who doesn't want to talk about these things is someone you are better off without.

SOME TESTS YOU CAN RUN ON ANY PARTNER TO SCREEN FOR PAST JERK BEHAVIOR

1) **Always ask early on about your date's past, especially his history of relationships and his history with the police.** See how he reacts to these questions. If he is evasive or very general in his comments, he may be hiding something. On the other hand, he

may tell stories with pride regarding how he got away with things or how the police were stupid and how he cleverly fooled them. In either case, listen carefully both for the content (what did he actually do) and the style of presentation. If he has a long list of aggressive offenses, such as assault, child abuse, domestic abuse, robbery, use of weapons, drug sales, and so forth, make this your last date.

Listen also to how he tells the story. Does he blame others for his behavior? Does he minimize the effect that he had on others? Does he try to convince you that it wasn't that bad, was a long time ago, or that he was framed? You are looking for a willingness to take responsibility for his past bad behavior. A person who has a lot of excuses and explanations is a bad bet as a partner.

If there are just a couple offenses and they're a long time back, listen to the explanation. Listen for signs of remorse, responsibility for the effect on others, and concrete steps that he took to change his attitude and behavior. Did he get clean through treatment? Did he come to recognize why he acted that way and find another way to meet his needs? Did he get into counseling or a religious practice or a support group or do something that helped him change directions?

People do change, but they don't change by magic. A person with a criminal past may have reformed, but you should ask for evidence of how and why he is different now. If you don't, you may end up as the victim of his next crime.

One other small tip, but it can be a life saver: find out if this person has any aliases. People who go by more than one name are almost always into something they don't want to get caught at. A person with multiple aliases should be scratched off your contact list immediately. It is almost certain they are a criminal thinker.

2) Always ask early on about other relationships. Find out how they started and how they ended, and what his attitude was about them. You are looking for signs that he viewed his partner as an equal, that he takes responsibility for his contributions to the demise of the relationship, and that he worked to learn something from it. Get names if you can, and if it's anyone you know or have a relationship with or can find a way to contact, don't hesitate to call them up and ask them how things went, no matter how bad he says she was. Ask especially about the beginning and ending, and compare notes. Did he come on as a charmer at first? Did he want to get involved really quickly? Did he seem to want to run the show all the time? Was he dishonest in ways she didn't see at first? See how their story checks out with what he says and does. And if he really doesn't want you to talk to the ex, that tells you a lot as well.

If he describes a violent or difficult breakup, don't let him off the hook if he says that she was abusive. Almost every abuser I've known has characterized himself as the victim. It's a basic Jerk characteristic to see himself as being mistreated and misunderstood by the rest of the world, through no fault of his own. While it is possible that his partner was abusive, listen to how he describes it. Does he take any responsibility or does he just trash her? Does he wonder what he could have done differently, or does he blame her for everything that went wrong? Any downgrading or hostile comments about an ex, however well deserved they may be, indicate the need for extreme caution.

If he talks about having a restraining order on him, or them having mutual restraining orders, or he talks about the police being involved in the breakup, you absolutely *must* investigate further. Do NOT accept any excuses or explanations that "she set me up" or "we were both arrested but she attacked me" or "it was me that called the police and they busted me anyway." These are suspiciously irresponsible and blaming statements. Even if they are 100% true and accurate, the way they are stated reflects a lack of accountability for things having gotten to that condition. And the odds are pretty good that if he's got a restraining order against him, it's for a good reason.

3) Do a criminal record check. Especially if there are any red or even pink flags in sections 1) or 2) above, it is in your best interests to see his entire criminal history, including any 911 calls, arrests, charges, and convictions. Most places, you can get this done for a relatively small fee. Information regarding these facts is public record. It's not always possible to get the original police reports, but if you find any that you need to see, ask your potential partner to grant you access. If they balk at this, that would be good enough for me to dump them. I know this seems harsh, but this person has a criminal background and you need to protect yourself. If they are truly reformed, they ought to understand your desire to know about their past and to make sure they have changed. Any attempts to guilt-trip you with statements like, "Don't you trust me?" or "That was all in the past" or "I don't see why that matters – like I told you, I don't do that stuff anymore" are almost certain to indicate Jerky tendencies. I can see and understand a person being embarrassed about their past – you can acknowledge that, but remind him that you have had some bad experiences, too, and are just trying to be safe. If he can't understand that, you're better off without him.

If this idea makes you uncomfortable, ask yourself why it should? If you had been convicted of beating up someone, would it surprise you if the Nanny agency wanted to know what happened before they hired you? If you were hiring someone to work for a bank, and he had an embezzlement history, wouldn't you want to know exactly what happened before you considered taking him on? And if he refused to give you that information, saying you should trust him and that was all in the past, would you not instantly scratch him off your list of potential employees?

Of course, there is also the question as to why you'd ever want to consider someone who has a criminal history of interpersonal crimes as a date. You probably wouldn't even think about hiring the embezzler, no matter what his police reports said. Why would you want to go out with someone who has beaten up his partner, no matter what the reason? Anyone who would physically beat on a partner is a Jerk with a capital "J"! But at a minimum, you need to know EXACTLY what happened if there was an incident that he was arrested or charged for, even if the charges were dropped or he was acquitted.

A comment about charges and convictions. It is rare that an abuser is actually charged with a crime. Most victims of domestic assaults are afraid to even call the police. If they do call, the perpetrator is often able to avoid being arrested by agreeing to leave the premises, or accusing her of being the abuser, or sometimes running before the police arrive. If there is an arrest, most of the time, the victim is unwilling to testify, either due to fear of retaliation (which is often quite justified), or due to the Jerk worming his way back in with apologies and veiled threats so that the victim is talked out of taking a hard stand. If there are actual charges filed, it usually means things have gotten pretty dangerous and the victim is desperate for some protection.

When there are charges filed, abusers can often get off with a plea bargain to a "lesser charge." It is amazingly common that major abusive Jerks will tell you, "I was innocent, but I agreed to the plea because I knew the courts would screw me over if I went to trial." This kind of statement is almost never true. There are situations where a person is pressured into making admissions, but it is very rare in domestic abuse cases, in my experience. To the contrary, domestic abusers generally get off way too easily when compared to someone who did the same thing to a total stranger. If I assaulted a female stranger and sent her to the hospital, odds are I'd do some jail time. But domestic abusers are usually offered probation and a "batterer program" in lieu of jail time for the same offense. So whatever they are charged with is usually less than what was actually known to have happened, and what is known is generally a tiny bit of all that occurred leading up to the police call. In other words, if someone admitted to a charge, you have to assume that they were guilty. It would take a pretty amazing explanation to be good enough to convince me otherwise.

Finally, even someone being found "not guilty" does not mean they didn't do it. Think of the OJ Simpson trial. Most everyone thought he was guilty, but there some doubt entered in due to possible evidence tampering by the police. If that one possible explanation can't be eliminated, the person is acquitted of the crime. If the charges actually went to trial, it means the prosecutor was pretty confident that they could prove the perpetrator did as he was charged. I'm not saying innocent people don't get taken to trial and even convicted, because they certainly do. But I am saying that the fact that someone was found "not guilty" does not mean they were innocent.

To summarize this section, don't be shy about demanding full information about any criminal charges, arrests, or even 911 calls. Odds are great that this is only the tip of the iceberg. It's not distrustful to check these things out – it's just plain smart. A person with a history of assault, rape, child abuse, or domestic abuse of any kind is a very bad risk. And if you are too worried about his reaction to even ask, it's definitely time to look for greener pastures.

4) Check also for civil restraining orders. These are also public record and should be available at your local courthouse. Any order that restrains him from contacting a past partner, or contacting his own children or stepchildren, needs full and thorough investigation. Again, he ought to expect this, and while it might be irritating or embarrassing, he should cooperate fully as you look into what this might mean for you. If he won't, or if what he says does not jibe with what you find out from other sources, dump him right away. As stated above, it takes a lot to get to the point of a restraining order being filed, and what is stated in the order is probably a small fraction of what actually happened. Again, it is true that there are such things as false restraining orders, but they are pretty rare and should check out upon investigation. You are doing nothing wrong by checking these things out, and if he "doesn't understand" why you need to know, that's probably enough to identify him as Jerk material without even knowing what happened.

5) If he is involved with the child welfare system or is restricted to only supervised visits with his kids by a court, again, you need to know all the details. This almost never happens without a reason, and while courts can be biased and make poor decisions, you will want to see for yourself what the issues are and get some data from other sources besides your partner. If he's on the up-and-up, his story will make sense and check out with others. Once again, an unwillingness to help you explore this area is a bad sign in itself – if he's innocent he'll want you to know the whole story. If he's reluctant, odds are he has something to hide.

6) Check for psychiatric hospitalizations. I am the last one to think that a mental illness diagnosis means that a relationship is doomed – there are many, many successful relationships where one or both parties suffer from mental or emotional challenges. But you will want to know why the person was in the hospital to see if it is connected to Jerkish tendencies.

The reasons for hospitalizations are almost always a danger to self or others. Find out which it was. If they were a danger to others, find out why and to whom he was a danger, and check for what is different now. Get verification from others as to what happened and what has changed. See if it was a single incident or happened more than once, if substance abuse was involved, and whether someone was hurt. Most Jerks are not mentally ill at all, but it can happen that they run afoul of the criminal justice system and sometimes can use "mental health problems" as a way to avoid other consequences. It's not a deal breaker, but should be taken very seriously.

In particular, watch for the "I was off my meds" excuse. If that's the reason, why was he "off his meds"? Is he unable to control himself without taking psychiatric drugs? If so, what is to stop him from "going off his meds" again? And what else is he doing besides taking drugs to try and deal with his mental health problems? A person whose *only* strategy to deal with emotional problems is psychiatric drugs may not be taking a lot of responsibility and may readily blame his psychiatrist or the wrong medication for his problems. Without getting into issues of mental health treatment, which would fill another book, the most important factor is whether the person is taking responsibility for finding solutions. Psychiatric drugs can reduce symptoms but don't create a better life by themselves. As always, you are looking for a sign of recognition that they have a problem and are responsible for fixing it. Any tendency to put the blame for their condition outside of their own control is reason to be worried.

The other thing to watch out for is the suicidal Jerk. Sometimes abusers will feign suicidal intentions as a way to get a victim not to leave. After all, who could leave someone in the middle of a mental health crisis? "What if he killed himself, it would be all my fault!" It's a great tactic that the more passive-aggressive Jerk will use when his victim is vulnerable to it. So look into any suicide attempts or threats and find out if they happened in the context of a breakup. If so, you need to investigate this very thoroughly, including talking to the ex about what happened. You also want to listen again for signs of responsibility – was it all her fault he tried to kill himself, or was it a bad decision on his part? If it was a bad decision, what was it based on and what evidence is there that he wouldn't do the same again faced with a similar situation? There are real suicidal people out there and they should certainly not be excluded from having a relationship with you just because they may struggle with suicidal feelings. But watch out for anyone who uses suicide to get their way. It is a sure sign that they will want to control everything and will use whatever tactics are necessary to assure you go along with their plans.

7) Check his attitude toward weapons. If he just collects old bullets or Civil War artifacts, no problem. But if he's obsessed with weaponry, watch out! I'd be particularly worried if he keeps loaded weapons out, and is resistant to locking up his weapons or ammo. If he thinks he needs weapons to fend off possible criminals, I'd consider it a very bad sign – he is fantasizing about shooting people. If he has committed a crime with a weapon, AND has weapons around, don't bother to ask further – you want out!

8) Ask others who know him about his personality. In particular, watch out for indications of a "temper" or "anger problems," as well as any history of violence or suicidal attempts in the context of a relationship. One person saying he has problems could be dismissed (unless it's a former partner!) but multiple people with the same opinion should not be ignored. A person with a reputation for temper control issues, especially in relation to a partner, should be avoided like the proverbial plague. Also, if your own children don't like him, or other kids seem to want to avoid him, pay attention – kids are often sensitive to nonverbal behavior that adults will not notice or will choose to dismiss. In fact, if there are kids around who know him, ask what they think of him. Their answers could be very enlightening.

In summary, there is no reason to shy away from fully investigating any problems or issues your partner may have had in the past. A person who is genuinely reformed may not be proud of his past, but he won't be afraid of you knowing about it and will have learned the lessons it has provided.

Remember that talk is cheap. Anyone can say they regret their past decisions, when often the only thing they actually regret is getting caught. Look beyond words to the actions this person has taken to change their life for the better. While people do make youthful mistakes and do grow up, it's up to you to make sure that those past actions don't extend into the present. Someone Jerky in their youth doesn't just stop being a Jerk because they get older. It takes recognizing the problem and learning to act differently. Don't just believe someone who says they have changed or who blames their past indis-cretions on others or on circumstances they didn't control.

And if your partner gets upset with you for asking and decides not to go out with you anymore, consider yourself lucky. Chances are about a thousand to one that you just sent a Jerk looking for a more willing victim.

CHAPTER 11

Addiction/Substance Abuse

LARRY WAS A MARIJUANA USER WHEN ANNIE MET HIM AS AN ADULT. She'd long ago decided that marijuana use was a deal-breaker for her. Larry promised to quit, and did so for some time. But once he'd gotten her to move across the country with him, his marijuana use returned. She also discovered that he was a heavy drinker, a fact he'd disguised from her during his intense courtship.

Mark not only sold marijuana and other drugs to teens to finance his college education, he continued to smoke dope regularly as an adult. When he found out Jan didn't smoke and disapproved, he actually tried to talk her into changing her mind and joining him when he smoked.

Addictive Behaviors

Many Jerks engage in a wide range of addictive behaviors. This can include substance abuse, gambling, excessive spending, pornography, video games, overeating, promiscuity, or any other repetitive activity that makes them feel temporarily better with a minimum of thought or labor. So screening for addiction is an absolute must in anybody's Jerk detection strategy.

Why are Jerks so likely to also be addicted to substances or destructive behaviors? Well, if you remember in Chapter 6, we identified that the one characteristic most Jerks have in common is a lack of responsibility. It is to be expected that a person who is not willing to admit that he creates his own physical and emotional reality will look for the easy way out when he is feeling bad. In other words, when they experience negative feelings or consequences from their prior decisions, rather than look for the source of the problem and take responsibility for handling the cause, most Jerks simply look for a way to make the pain go away.

> In all the time I knew my husband he never went one day without having an alcoholic drink, and it was not just a glass of wine with his meal. He would drink an awful lot, but he was never drunk as such. I think he had so much tolerance to the stuff it no longer affected him. My parents always blamed the drink for the way he treated me, but I have since learned that drink does not cause anyone to be abusive. He also got highly defensive when I spoke to him about it and even more defensive and really angry when he heard I had spoken to others about it once…
>
> I would definitely say it is a bad sign if they can drink a lot of alcohol and it has no real effect, because it means they are deadening what is inside. That is never a good sign.
>
> –FS

When Is It an Addiction?

Any of the addictive behaviors listed above can be engaged in within reasonable limits and not be an indicator of trouble. It's OK to go out drinking once in a while, or have a glass of wine with your dinner. There's nothing wrong with playing the lottery for fun, or going on the occasional shopping spree, or eating a huge meal when you know you are on a diet. Video games can be lots of fun, and having the occasional sexual fling is not inherently harmful. And lots of healthy adults find pornography interesting or stimulating without letting it take over their lives.

What you are looking for here is obsession. An addictive gambler doesn't just like to gamble for fun, they feel they NEED to gamble. They spend a large amount of time and money gambling, and even when they experience negative consequences, they don't feel they can stop. Gambling eventually may stop even being fun, but the addicted person can't seem to do without it. He may make promises to himself or others to cut down or stop, but these are generally short lived. He may also start to lie to others or himself about what he's doing, or try to minimize the impact of his behavior to make himself feel a little better.

Any of the other behaviors can be regarded in the same way. A person who eats excessively whenever he feels bad, even if he gains a lot of weight or exacerbates his diabetes or risks a heart attack, is behaving in an addictive fashion. A porn addict doesn't just dabble – he's using porn all the time, losing sleep, spending lots of money, losing friends, getting in trouble or fired from a job, and yet continues the behavior. An alcoholic or drug addict continues to use despite getting arrested for DUI, getting in a car accident, being too hung over to go to work, undermining his health, and alienating friends and family.

> Mike would get his paycheck and blow the money. I found out he is a gambler. He took me to the casino. He bought two one-hundred dollar tokens. He dropped one one-hundred dollar token in machine. He lost. He picked up his second and last one-hundred dollar token. His hand was reaching towards the machine. I said "don't do it!" He had this insane look in his eye while his hand trembled as he reached to drop the token in machine. That was all the money from his paycheck! I realized that it controlled him. He then relied on me to support him through the week. He didn't help out, 'cause he said he works!!!
>
> –Anonymous

> He would make me watch porn with him; I hated it, as it

would make me feel uncomfortable and sick to my core with some of the violent movies. I realise now, many years later, that he in fact acted out a lot of the aggressive, some times violent sexual acts that he saw in these movies. He needed sex all the time; at our engagement party he pulled me upstairs in my parents' house to have sex in the hallway while everyone else was downstairs. I was so scared someone would find us. Another time we had sex in my parents' bed, to me that was the ultimate in degrading my parents. He thought it was funny. When we were dating we would go to a park down the road from my house and have sex in the car then he would drive me home.

–AS, 56, Australia, 13 years married

So an addiction is a compulsive use of a behavior to make yourself feel better or keep from feeling worse, despite negative consequences directly relating to this behavior. It really can include any behavior at all that interferes with daily functioning. And while many addicts are not specifically Jerks, Jerks are very commonly addicts who engage in multiple examples of compulsive behavior.

Addiction vs. Jerkiness

There are a couple of points I want to make very clear. First, there are a lot of reasons that people become addicted to various behaviors that are not related to Jerky attitudes. As it happens, a lot of victims of abuse turn to drugs or alcohol to dampen the pain they don't feel they can otherwise manage. Physical illness, losing a job, the death of a loved one, feelings of loneliness and isolation, or even a lack of purpose or direction in life, all can get people started down the path to addiction. So being addicted to something is not the same as being a Jerk, even though they are highly associated.

Which leads to the second and even more important point: substance abuse does NOT cause abusive behavior! (Although it has been shown to lead to more serious violence in cases where abuse issues are present.) While abuse perpetrators are more likely to abuse substances, this is generally regarded as being a symptom of the abusive personality, rather than the cause. In other words, Jerks are both more likely to abuse substances AND to abuse people.

> He drank, man he drank, he used the drink to excuse the violence and abuse. He sobbed he had a problem with drinking, please could I not just support him this once? Took me to his anti-drink classes so I could see him lie to everyone, how they all believed him.... After I left him, he turned to abusing his family, and died of drink-related bleeding into the brain at the grand age of 42, leaving so many lives shattered.
>
> –C, 36, abused 4½ years

There are many examples in the news and in movies, TV and novels where abusive behavior is shown as the result of substance abuse, and the person in question suddenly becomes loving and normal once they stop drinking or using drugs. I can't say that this never happens, but in my experience, Jerks who stop using drugs generally start in on or continue a range of other addictive behaviors and continue to be Jerks. The substance abuse is the result of their Jerky, no-responsibility attitude toward life, not the cause, and stopping the substances without changing the irresponsible attitude does little to help the victim of a Jerk who happens to be an addict.

Characteristics of Addiction

A couple of other comments about addiction before we return to how this applies to your Jerk screening process. It is important to note that an addict doesn't necessarily engage in this behavior every day. There are chronic addicts who may not drink or gamble or spend in huge outbursts, but will not be able to go a day without a little "hit" of their pain-relieving activity. But there are others who "binge" – they may only drink a couple of times a month, but when they do, they get totally wasted and black out and crash the car. Or they may only gamble once in a while, but are capable of losing thousands at one drop. The key to look for is a loss of control – they feel they HAVE to continue the behavior despite the fact that it is harmful, even if the damage is intermittent and they otherwise function reasonably well between bouts.

Prescription Drug Abuse

The other thing to be aware of is that prescription drug abuse is on the rise. There are more and more addicts who have learned how to go to a doctor and tell them the right symptoms to get a prescription painkiller or anxiety relief drug. And many doctors are all too willing to write a prescription for an addictive drug without considering the possibility that the person is using the drug inappropriately. Awareness of this trend is increasing among professionals in recent years, but it's still pretty easy for a prescription drug addict to get what he needs legally, and even get his insurance to pay for it.

Typical addictive drugs to watch out for are painkillers (such as Oxycodone, Codeine, Vicodin) and anti-anxiety drugs (such as Valium, Xanax, Klonopin). It is fairly easy to pretend to suffer pain or anxiety, or to use the genuine experience of either to justify drug prescriptions that the user can then increase the dosage of, or use in the binging fashion described above. The use of any of these addictive substances for longer than a few weeks at a time is probably something you want to look into further, as it may indicate an unidentified addiction. The fact that a drug is prescribed doesn't mean the person is not abusing the drug.

> My ex was addicted to opiates (specifically heroin, though he abused prescription pills, too) and video games. He also was a self-proclaimed sex-addict.
> Huge red flag at the beginning of the relationship

was that he told me he "used" to have a substance abuse problem but was not working on any program. I figured since he had a good job, was clean cut, and didn't fit the idea that I had created of what a heroin addict was, I thought "Oh he must be OK." The truth was, he was using drugs from day one, and it spiraled out of control by 6 months into the relationship. Other red flags later on included – spent way too much money, went to work early and came home late but never had the money to account for working so much, would become MIA for long periods of time by not answering his phone, lied, had track marks, didn't have much of a sex drive, nodding off, withdrawals (getting sick a lot), etc.

–SA

So that's addiction – a compulsive behavior that a person relies on to feel better or avoid feeling bad. Such addictions can vary from mild to severe, and not all addicted people are Jerks, nor are all Jerks addicts. But the use of addictive behaviors to keep uncomfortable feelings at bay is very common for Jerks, because it allows them to avoid or defer taking responsibility for their current condition.

My husband was "unable" to have sex with me as he had trouble obtaining an erection. I chalked it up to his age (54 – when a lot of men start having trouble). However, I noticed that when I would return home, he had been on my computer and was always looking up pornography. I used to click on it to see what he was looking up and found disturbing amounts of clicking on "she-males, cross dressing and barely legal age teen." When I questioned him about this, he always just said that it was curiosity and that he didn't do it, etc.…

–BK

Is He an Addict?

So how do you tell the difference between addiction and normal behavioral variations that you might personally not find attractive? And more importantly, how can you evaluate whether addictive behavior is simply a problem in itself or an indicator of a more serious set of Jerky attitudes and behavior?

The first thing to look at is the behavior itself – how do you know if it is an addiction or an abuse of a behavior or substance? Here are some key questions: Is it something they engage in only on rare occasions? Or is it something they feel they have to do all the time? Do they appear to be having fun doing it? Or do they show signs of frustration with or craving for the addiction, either during the compulsive behavior or between episodes? If it's a binging type of behavior, does it seem to be getting more frequent or more intense over time? Do they keep it secret from you or are they willing to share the details of what they do and why?

Have negative consequences occurred, such as bank overdrafts, health problems, criminal charges, loss of a job or money-making opportunity, or loss of a significant relationship? Have these consequences had any impact on the behavior? Have there been unsuccessful attempts to cut down or quit? Unsuccessful attempts at treatment?

> Alcohol – ended up with dementia, liver damage, and heart damage (and one hell of a bulbous ugly nose – ha ha). Food – could not stop eating – ate about a kilo of chocolate a day. Television – once it was on, it didn't go off. Pornography (in the early days he spoke disparagingly about men who did it, but he was doing it the whole time – the more degrading and violent, the better). He once complained to a mutual friend that one of our biggest problems was that I didn't like pornography. Frotteurism [rubbing against others for sexual gratification] – got him into a lot of trouble, at work, in public, and on

our social scene. The Internet – he got on the computer at 6:30 am and did not often get off until 1 am. He got up to eat, or to take a walk, or make dinner (although the Internet was often on while he was cooking as his laptop was on the counter). He just never stopped.

Now someone please tell me why he wasn't addicted to fixing cars, cleaning, doing the gardening, or renovating?? Why aren't THOSE common addictions?

–TK, 59, Canada, abused 10 years

The preceding questions are all aimed at whether the behavior in question qualifies as an addiction. Of course, there is a whole spectrum of addictive behavior, and there is no black and white line that says this behavior is acceptable whereas that one counts as addiction. But the main characteristic of addiction is the tendency to continue the behavior despite destructive consequences.

So let's say you have determined that yes, this person is a shop-a-holic or a sex addict or is hooked on meth. Is that a deal breaker in itself? Only you can decide this, but significant addiction is a red flag of the most serious kind. If it's a person you've known for a while, you may want to give him a chance to get it together before you call things off. If the addiction appears relatively mild or benign, such as watching too much football on Sunday afternoons, you may decide it's something you can live with. But my general advice would be to stay away from a committed relationship with a person in a seriously addictive pattern of behavior. I've seen too many lives destroyed when partners or family members waited around hoping for a miracle. And I have seen addicts turn around, but generally only when they've been allowed to fall on their faces and suffer serious consequences for their addictive behavior. Trying to "help" such a person by paying their bills, bailing them out of jail, giving them a place to live, fixing their tickets, or trying to find them a job almost always leads to you feeling taken advantage of and the addiction becoming deeper. The best message you can give such a person is, "I care enough about you not to support your addictive behavior. I would be happy to support you in getting help, but I won't be here to watch you destroy yourself. You'll have to do that on your own."

Is He Also a Jerk?

There is a huge overlap between typical behaviors that an addict (especially a substance abusing addict) engages in and what we have described as a typical Jerk. So how do you tell the difference between someone who is acting badly as a result of their addiction and someone who is a chronic Jerk who happens also to be abusing substances or gambling or engaging in some other addictive behavior?

A few things come to mind. First off, an addict is spending most of his/her time seeking the addictive substance or behavior. They often don't really care that much about relationships or the feelings of others, which is a lot like a Jerk, but their focus is the addiction, not you. In contrast, a Jerk will be focused on controlling your behavior in addition to whatever addiction they're stuck in. For instance, a lot of Jerks will blame their abusive behavior on alcohol: "I only hit you because I was wasted." "It was the drink talking, not me." "You shouldn't have said that, you knew I was high." Or my favorite, "I was drunk, I don't remember what happened."

It's amazing how many "blackouts" conveniently coincide with an abusive incident. But consider for a moment: if you had been really drunk and blacked out, and found out later that you'd hit or beaten your partner, what would you do? Would you say, "Gosh, I was just drunk. You know how I get?" I doubt it. A healthy person would feel devastated! They'd wonder how they could possibly have engaged in such a behavior, drunk or sober, and if they felt drinking was in any way connected with this loss of responsibility, they'd make sure they had a plan to stop drinking, or at least never get that drunk again! So the sign you are looking for is not that they got drunk, or even blacked out, but what they did while drunk, and what their attitude toward it is afterwards. A Jerk will generally be willing to blame the drink for his violence or infidelity or gambling losses, and will expect you to either accept or automatically forgive his behavior as being out of character. He will assure you his behavior was caused by the drinking, rather than a result of his own attitude and beliefs coming out when his inhibitions were lowered by being drunk.

As an illustration of this, let me share a personal story. When I was about 16, I went through a phase of occasional binge drinking, driven by my personal anxiety and desire to fit in. On one occasion, I drank enough to black out for a while, and literally didn't remember what happened for several hours. When I asked my brothers later what had happened, they described my ironic and (to them) very amusing efforts to keep another kid from driving home drunk while being hardly able to talk myself.

My attitudes and beliefs center around helping others and being responsible. Even in a totally blacked out state of near unconsciousness, my first impulse was to take responsibility for protecting someone else. Alcohol didn't suddenly fill me with an urge to beat someone up. Admittedly, if I'd been sober, I doubt I would have had the nerve to try to talk to someone about driving home drunk. So getting wasted definitely reduced my fears and inhibitions. But what I was inhibiting was an urge to help and protect, not an urge to hit or destroy.

So don't ever accept an explanation that your partner was abusive because he was drunk. If drinking took away his inhibitions, it means he was thinking about being abusive while sober but was able to restrain himself. Which means the abusive impulse is still there when he's sober. And the truth is, he most likely wasn't blacked out at all – he just told you that to avoid taking responsibility for what he did.

Now I don't want you to have to wait until he attacks you in a drunken stupor to check him out on this point. So how do you find this out without direct evidence? Pretty easy – you ask him to tell you about times he was drunk, high, or otherwise impaired, and see how he relates the tale. While there is often a macho male "pride" in being "really wasted," a non-abusive person is unlikely to boast of beating someone up or otherwise being aggressive and foolish while under the influence. If he appears to be a drinker or habitual drug user, if you haven't already eliminated him from consideration, ask some friends and family what he's like when he gets drunk or high. If people say things like, "He's a mean drunk," you know all you need to know. Get away now, because a mean drunk is most likely a mean person trying to pretend he's not mean until intoxication robs him of the ability to mask his true personality.

Similar tests can be used for other addictive behavior. Did he gamble because he was drunk? Because he was depressed? Because he'd lost money last night and was "due for a break?" Look for irresponsible statements that suggest the gambling is caused by something other than his personal choice to gamble. Same for compulsive spending, sex, or other behavior that appears to be out of control. Check always for responsibility. "I knew I was spending more than I wanted to, but I decided to just let myself and to economize next week," is much more responsible than, "I don't know what got hold of me – I just lost track of how much I'd spent." Or "I just wanted a quick fling, even though I know it's not great for me emotionally. It felt better for the night and I was willing to deal with the aftermath," rather than, "She was just so gorgeous, I couldn't help myself" or "She was totally coming on to me, what was I supposed to do?" The addictive behavior may be a problem in itself (for instance, you may appropriately be very strong about expecting sexual fidelity in relationships), but that is more of an issue of your personal values and priorities. The behavior becomes more of a red flag when the perpetrator starts blaming others (or the addiction itself) for making him act the way he did.

> I never thought about it as an addiction, but my husband
> was when I met him and still is a total work-a-holic. Every
> second of the day is consumed by his work. He is also self
> employed.… And as well, he over extends himself to the
> point that his attitude is that he is doing everything and
> no one helps him, even though I am right there helping
> him. I feel he has spite for us, the kids and I, that he has
> to work so hard to support our family.
>
> –L

Secrecy

As we saw in Chapter 6, lying and minimizing are also very common
Jerk characteristics, and should be checked for if any addictive
behavior pattern is noticed. If a partner is at least honest about
the behavior, it provides some chance for discussion. For instance,
a person who smokes openly makes it easy to decide if you are
willing to put up with that due to his other positive attributes. It
also makes it more possible for him to address the issue if you do
tell him it's a deal breaker for you. Though I wouldn't count on it,
an open attitude toward addictive behavior allows the possibility
that the addicted person may be motivated to change. But if the
behavior is secret, you may never know it exists, let alone whether
it's actually changing in accordance to some promise or agreement
that has been made. This becomes all the more critical with more
destructive behavior, such as drug and alcohol abuse, sexual infidelity, and gambling. If you find that $500 has come up missing,
your partner acts baffled, and you discover later that he gambled
it away on video poker but didn't want you to know, you are in
very deep trouble and had better get out of there immediately. At
least an overt addiction can be seen and talked about, but a secret
one is a problem that is very unlikely to ever be addressed. And
as we already know, lying is a common abuser characteristic that

should make you very cautious. Combine lying with serious addictive behavior, and there's no need to look further – this person has got to go!

> He gambled heavily. I noticed scratch-off tickets were piled high on the floor of our van. I didn't know this was serious gambling until he leaped to his death off the casino parking structure years later....
>
> He would steal money from my house, and he blamed my kids for the missing money. He would use my check card at the ATM and he double-dipped transactions. His explanation was someone must have been peeking over his shoulder and got the password. Of course I questioned this nonsense. He would explode and scream that I always accuse him. He would scream that my kids run me over. His face got so crazy and red faced that all I could do was calm him down. And he got away with it again.
>
> **–Anonymous**

Of course, you will want to check for the level of consequences that your potential partner has already endured and compare them to current behavior, as we discussed in the last chapter. Look for multiple instances of the same consequence – multiple arrests, multiple relationship failures, multiple job losses, multiple financial emergencies, etc. If you see this kind of pattern and you see addictive behavior, odds are the two are related and both will probably persist. If he claims he's changed, refer to the last chapter on how to screen for someone giving lip service vs. real changes in behavior.

Some Simple Ways to Check for Addictive Behavior and its Connection to Other Jerk Indicators

1) Screen EVERY relationship for any addictive tendencies.
We all have a few habitual behavior patterns – find out what they are and how "hooked" the person is to the behavior. Think very broadly about what the person may be addicted to. Key questions to ask are: What does this person do every single day as a matter of habit? And what does this person do under stress? Look for healthy attitudes or patterns toward stress management. Does the person have a range of possible responses? Do they recognize their "addictions" for what they are? Are they able to redirect their attention from these patterns when necessary? Is there anything they do that seems to detract from their welfare, and yet they continue to do it despite adverse consequences?

2) ANY sign of substance abuse is to be taken very seriously, regardless of how "nice" the person is otherwise or what substance he is abusing. If a person drinks regularly, find out how much and how often? A person who has a beer or glass of wine every night at dinner is not abusing alcohol. A person who has three to four every night probably is. A person who has six every night is almost certainly a chronic alcoholic and should be avoided until and unless they give it up and get some help with their life priorities. And don't ever accept "it's only beer" as a rationalization. My uncle drank a six-pack every night, only beer, never during the daytime, and died at 44 as a result of his alcoholism. Beer can be a serious addiction, and anyone trying to convince you otherwise is justifying behavior that is probably destructive.

As to other substances, I'd say any illegal drug use at all is a deal breaker. Marijuana may be an exception in some people's minds, but I'd still apply what I said about alcohol to marijuana. Anybody who smokes marijuana every day for non-medical reasons is addicted and needs to get help. And don't accept "medical reasons" without scrutiny, either. Remember how easy it is to say, "I'm in pain," and get a prescription. Check out the usage pattern and intent. It may not seem as bad as getting drunk every day, but in the long run, the results end up being similar – negative consequences include increasing dependence, driving errors and citations, job losses, loss of motivation, financial losses, and other legal complications, as well as chronic health issues that can be devastating. Not to mention the fact that using marijuana or any drug to cope with day-to-day living frequently indicates a lack of responsibility for one's own condition that, as we said in Chapter 6, correlates strongly with abusive behavior. A lot of Jerks smoke dope.

Don't forget to check for prescription drug abuse as well. In addition to the usual signs, watch out for anyone who takes someone else's prescription or buys, sells, gives away or trades prescription drugs in any way. Other red flags include taking more than the dosage that is required, going to more than one doctor for prescriptions for vague complaints like "anxiety" or "chronic pain," having multiple prescriptions for the same kind of drug at the same time, or using the hospital emergency room to get treatment for non-emergency conditions (it's easier to get a prescription for an "emergency" and the doctors at the ER aren't as able to cross-check what other treatment they are receiving). Even though they are legal, many prescription drugs are addictive and should be considered a danger sign, especially if combined with other "Jerk Radar" signs that we have already discussed.

3) For any addictive behavior, look to see what negative consequences have ensued and how the person has responded to these. Have they gotten a DUI arrest? Did this have any effect on their drinking? Have they been arrested for possession or sale of illegal drugs? Do they continue to justify the behavior despite the consequences? Have they had injuries or illnesses connected with the drugs? Have they been fired from a job as a result of absences or conflicts with superiors? Has any of this altered their behavior or caused them to seek treatment or therapy of some kind?

Other addictive behavior that does not involve substance abuse can still have adverse consequences that you can check for. Even something as silly as computer games (this is one of mine) can lead to loss of sleep, getting written up on the job for playing "Solitaire" during work hours, or missing out on other fun activities due to obsession about the game. For compulsive gambling or spending, the obvious sign is high debt levels. Other consequences could be the loss of relationships with spouse or family members over gambling, the loss of physical health due to stress, prior bankruptcies, etc. Food addictions could lead to being overweight or underweight, having disrupted relationships due to eating patterns, and having other adverse health consequences such as liver problems or heart issues or diabetes. Compulsive porn viewing could cause rifts in the marital relationship, loss of sleep, loss of interest in normal sexual activity, being busted on the job for looking at porn, or spending excessive amounts of money on porn movies or sites. Look at any addictive behavior and see if the person is continuing the behavior despite these adverse consequences.

The above three checks are only about discovering if the person has an addictive behavior pattern. Lots of non-Jerks have addictions and need help in getting them under control, and you should make sure they get that help before you commit to a long-term relationship. But from here on out, we'll look at how addiction can relate to other Jerk factors that you want to screen for.

4) Ask him to tell you some stories about his addictive behaviors. Is he embarrassed, or does he sound proud of being "so wasted"? Does he think it's funny that he did something really stupid or aggressive when drunk or high? Does he think other people are funny when they do stupid or aggressive things when drunk or high? His attitude toward intoxicated behavior will tell you a lot about his internal beliefs about addiction. An addict may be compulsive and need intervention to help him stop drinking. A Jerk generally doesn't really see the need to stop.

5) Check very thoroughly for any tendency to explain away behavior as happening "because I was wasted." Especially when combined with the attitude of pride or humor I just described, this is almost a sure sign you're in for big trouble. Even if it's relatively small, such as an insulting remark or accidentally knocking someone's drink to the floor, a normal person will be embarrassed or feel remorseful and try to do something to make up for the damage. I remember in high school hearing someone talking with humor about how they were so drunk, they drove up on the sidewalk by accident and ran over someone's garden fence. They told it as a funny story, and apparently made no effort to go back and fix it or pay the person for the damage done. This kind of irresponsibility is totally characteristic of a Jerk and should be challenged at the very lowest level. If the person gets irritated at you for asking him, "Did you pay for the damage?" or responds, "Hell, no! What kind of fool do you think I am?" you'd better get rid of them ASAP. But really, do you want someone in your life who gets drunk enough to drive on the sidewalk? Or who thinks it's funny to do so?

6) Look for significant behavior changes that this person shows when engaged in his addictive behavior. Do they become aggressive, irritable, moody, withdrawn, lazy, irresponsible? Remember that substances, in particular, don't make a person act in a certain way, they tend to bring down our inhibitions and let us act the way we probably were already wanting to. A person who is "nice" to you but gets mean when drunk probably isn't nice at all. He is probably acting nice to win you over, but once the "honeymoon" is over, you'll start to see some of that mean behavior when he's stone cold sober.

7) See if the person blames "stress" or other life circumstances for his need to engage in the addictive behavior. A person who gets drunk because he had a bad day at work, or gambles because he needs money to pay the bills, or picks someone up at a bar because his "girlfriend wouldn't put out" is making excuses for continuing the behavior. This kind of low responsibility is almost surely a sign that your partner is a Jerk in disguise. Later on, you will find that your behavior or someone else's "forces" him to look at porn or spend money or get wasted and drive the car drunk. This kind of irresponsibility is the core of what makes a Jerk a Jerk. Don't allow it in your life!

8) Look for signs of lying or minimizing addictive behavior. A person who says, "I only drink on weekends" or "It was a party, I lost control of myself" or "I only had three" when he really had eight is a person who is working hard at convincing you and himself that he doesn't have a problem. If you think he's got a problem, probably the best test of all is to say so to his face, in a kind but direct fashion. "I notice you seem to drink every day." Or, "You told me you're short on food but bought a $1200 entertainment system this week. Can you explain to me how that works?" Or, "I noticed you just spent 14 hours in the last two days watching football, but you said the drain in your kitchen needed fixing. Could you have found some time to take a break and work on it?" You don't have to be mean about it, but just ask the question. In the answer, you want to be listening for any tendency to suggest that "it's not that bad" or "I don't do it all the time" or "don't worry, I have a big check coming in that will take care of that debt." More honest answers would be, "I agree, I do drink too often. I'm going to take a look at that." Or "I know, I shouldn't have spent it. I don't know why I make those dumb decisions!" Or, "Yes, I should have fixed it. Sometimes I get hooked on football and forget everything else. Where is my toolkit?"

None of these things suggest the addiction would be in any way fixed – they simply show that the person sees at least to some degree that his behavior may be a problem for him or someone else. Many Jerks would rather spend a week in jail than accept that they are doing something wrong. It's either not their fault, or not that bad, or sometimes it didn't even happen. "I don't drink every night." "Gosh, I've been with you about 10 times now and you were drunk every time." "Well, I always drink on dates but not at other times." "I see. I came over to your house last week during the afternoon and you were hanging out with your sister. You were drinking then, too." "Well, she likes to drink and I hated to have her drink alone." And so on. A full-scale Jerk could have this conversation for days and you could bring up a hundred examples of why you see this as an issue, and he'll lie or deny every one of them. You want to look beyond the addictive behavior toward the person's attitude toward it. If he doesn't even acknowledge the actual facts, let alone admit that it could be a problem, he is a lost cause and will bring you nothing but misery.

Now some Jerks, especially early in a relationship, will admit very readily that "I have a problem" with drinking, drugs, gambling, or whatever. Their strategy will often be to tell you "I'm working on it" or "I'm getting a handle on it" or "I'm planning to get myself into treatment." The simple test on this one is to say, "When?" or "What exactly are you doing to 'work on it?'" Whether you're dealing with a true Jerk or just a garden-variety addict, you will want to insist that they get into treatment or go to AA groups or turn themselves in to their PO and face the music on their criminal actions or cut up their credit cards or cancel their porn accounts or take whatever concrete steps are necessary to make improvements. Talk is very cheap, especially among addicts. If you're even willing to consider a relationship with an addict (which I would strongly discourage), insist on full treatment and concrete evidence of substantial change over time before you are willing to move forward. Anybody can say "I'm trying." You need to see results.

9) Attempts to involve you with the addictive behavior are particularly alarming. Someone using meth who wants you to try it is not only unaware of their own addiction, he's trying to take you down with him! A porn addict who wants you to start acting the way they do in the videos is potentially very dangerous (see Chapter 12 for more details). A gambling addict who wants you to gamble, too, and tries to make you feel guilty for disapproving or not playing along is trying to manipulate you into violating your own integrity. Run from any situation where someone is trying to entice or force or pressure you into engaging in any behavior you see as destructive or unproductive, even if it's something completely legal like cigarettes. A person who would try to get another person addicted to make himself feel better about continuing his addiction is sure to be a Jerk of the highest degree.

10) Finally, if any attempt to respectfully discuss or confront addictive behavior is met with verbal attacks or hostility, it's time to end things right away. It takes courage to bring up behavior in a partner that you are concerned about. Of course, you need to be sensitive in your approach, but any partner who can't view your efforts to help with respect (even if he doesn't like what you are saying) is more concerned with himself and his own needs than he ever will with you. It is also a sign that you will always be expected to accept or put up with whatever behavior he thinks is OK, and that he feels OK about attacking you verbally if you don't go along with his plans. This is a Jerk's bread and butter and a sure sign that he has no intention of changing a thing.

Serious addiction is disruptive to any relationship. Addiction combined with Jerkish tendencies can be incredibly dangerous. While it is very clear from the literature that addiction does not cause abusive behavior, substance abuse and sexual addiction in particular raise the likelihood of serious injury or death from abuse. Look for addictive behaviors early and confront them directly. Make sure they are fully handled before you ever get more deeply committed to a relationship. Bottom line, people generally don't change their behavior without a major life upheaval, and even then most people (and especially most Jerks) will fall quickly back into old patterns when the heat is off. If you can't live with their current behavior, look elsewhere for a partner. Don't ever stay with him to "help him" with his problem. Because if you're seeing the problem now, when he's putting his best foot forward to try and convince you he's a great guy, the odds are tremendous that once the "honeymoon" is over, his problem will become *your* problem and will consume your life.

Stay away from addicts!

CHAPTER 12

Sexual Obsession or Manipulation

MARK WAS VERY INTERESTED IN SEXUAL INVOLVEMENT WITH JAN, AND those romantic dates deteriorated within several weeks into mostly watching TV and having sex. When Jan noted this to him, his "so what" attitude became clear – he was quite OK with TV and sex as the main course in his romantic life. Jan decided that wasn't enough for her, and decided to declare a moratorium on sex until they got involved in some other outside activities. Mark was not very happy with this plan, and for the first time, she saw some of the anger she'd seen directed at his ex and his family members coming in her own direction.

Sex is one area where many Jerks will show their true colors relatively early in a relationship. Jerks are, by nature, self-centered. The area of sexuality provides a great opportunity to take personal pleasure in the physical sense, and is therefore often a big focus or goal in a relationship. Additionally, sex allows the Jerk to exercise a certain level of dominance in the relationship within the bounds of what is socially accepted. As we've already seen, cultural expectations as expressed through film, television, and popular music put a pretty heavy emphasis on the male as the dominant force in a sexual relationship. So it can be pretty easy for a Jerk to convince his female partner to go along with a scenario where he calls the shots in the sexual arena.

Quick Sexual Involvement

One of the earliest and easiest signs to detect is pressure to become sexually involved very quickly. A combination of subtle pressure and smooth talking can make you feel that you are somehow either out of line or missing out on something great if you want to take it at a pace you are comfortable with. Many Jerks are skilled at subtly manipulating you into believing that if you are not willing to give him what he wants, he'll go looking elsewhere for sexual satisfaction. If you are getting the message that he might reject you if you set a sexual boundary, you're almost certainly dating a Jerk.

For instance, you may have a lovely evening and contemplate a sexy good-night kiss on the doorstep. The Jerk will invite himself inside, even though you weren't planning on it. He may gently pressure you to spend "just a few more minutes" combined with some flattery: "I'd hate for this beautiful night to end" or "I bet you are a great decorator – I'd just love to see what your living room looks like" – you get the idea. If you insist and stick to your point, he may look hurt or disappointed, or keep talking to you to prolong the conversation for another attempt to get in the door.

> On our first date he insisted we went back to his place, I told him categorically that I wouldn't sleep with him and that I wouldn't be staying over. We were listening to music in the living room when he left the room. He called me from the bedroom and asked me to go & lie with him. I did. Things began getting steamy & he undressed and lay beneath the covers, again asking me to join him. I said I wouldn't be taking clothes off...anyway, somehow, I did end up staying the night and we had sex three times. From then on, whenever I was with him we had sex like rabbits, it became a routine.... If I was sick or tired or just not in the mood, it didn't matter...
>
> He even asked me if I felt able to say no to him if I didn't want to make love, when I told him I didn't like to

> say no because I didn't want to disappoint him, he said it
> was ok to say no. Next time I tried to say no, I was ignored
> and the sulk lasted for days…
>
> —CH

Now it's just possible that your date might really be having such a good time and he didn't want the night to end yet, and he is genuinely disappointed that you won't invite him in. That's not the problem. The problem comes when you make it clear you are done for the night and he won't take no for an answer. However sweetly he does it, if you find yourself feeling like you're somehow wrong for setting a boundary, you may be dealing with someone who is trying to control and manipulate you for sexual gain.

Similar reasoning applies at any point where you set a limit in the sexual arena. You let him know you are OK with some heavy petting, but not ready for intercourse just yet. A certain amount of temporary disappointment is understandable, but when the pressure turns on, however gentle or "nice," that you should change your mind after you've made yourself clear, your alarm bells should go off. You have a right to have your sexual boundaries respected.

In some cases, it can get quite overt. If you find yourself being accused of being a "cock tease" or being expected to "put out" because you "led him on" or he "gave you a lovely evening," you should need no further information in order to scratch his name from your address book. Anybody who feels you owe him sex because he bought you dinner and a movie is incredibly self-centered and doesn't deserve any further attention from you.

> At the start of our relationship, I did not want to rush
> the physical, but it was very important to him. He kept
> pushing it, and eventually said that if I did not have sex
> with him then this would be a great problem in the rela-
> tionship and it would not survive. This is alongside all the
> crap he told me about me being the one and the love
> of his life, etc. Looking back now I should have known.

Someone who truly loves you would not force this on you if you were not ready.

–FS

He wanted sexual involvement right away, but did hold off the pressure till the STD tests were in. One night, he showed up at my house in our early dating days when I had just stepped out of the shower, threw me on the bed, performed oral sex on me to my total surprise, stood up and said, "See!! THAT'S how good it's going to be with us." Why oh why oh why oh why did I not say, Well then, forget about it – if that's all you can do. Ten year hindsight. I think the key for me was that I was uncomfortable with the whole scene. Like, suddenly I look down and there he was. I didn't know what to do.

–TK, 59, Canada, abused 10 years

Sexual Boastfulness

Another early sign is boastfulness about sexual prowess or conquests. A guy who has to tell you how good he is in bed is almost certainly a narcissist – he's more concerned about his sexual performance "grade" than he is about how you might feel about your experience with him as a partner. Unless you're just looking for a casual fling, in which case his studies in the area might prove interesting, don't bother with someone who boasts about sexual performance.

Some Jerks also spend time talking to their friends about how many women they've had. They don't usually talk to you about these things, but if you listen to talk amongst his male friends, you may hear some stories that tell you he views women as objects or conquests rather than people. Looking at movie figures he admires can also give a clue. If he identifies with James Bond very closely, for instance, don't figure on any kind of long-term relationship.

And if he directly boasts to YOU about his conquests, FORGET IT! He's a Jerk for absolute certain.

> We drank a lot and partied and sex was just always the way the night ended. He lived with other guys at the time and I remember they would hoot & holler if [they] heard us upstairs. It was embarrassing. And, one time we had sex while others were sleeping in a loft with us and the next day I heard him and a friend talking about how they "locked eyes" as he was having sex with me and his friend with another girl. It made me feel so cheap. He told stories of his past sex life (hookers, strip clubs, girl-friends, farmers' daughters…) and he was just so blunt and if I appeared upset, he was all, "well, I'm not going to lie to you!"
>
> –CF, 35, Vermont, married 5 years

Obsession with Pornography

Another soft sign we've mentioned before is obsession with pornography. As most people are aware, men (and increasingly, women) do sometimes find pornography and erotica stimulating on occasion, and this is certainly not a criticism or political commentary judging people for doing so. What I'm talking about here is an obsession: significant amounts of time and/or money being spent on porn, to the point that it seems like an important part of his life.

There are two main reasons why this is a bad sign. First off, someone who spends a lot of time with porn may be prone to seeing women as fantasies rather than real people. Porn women do whatever the man wants and ALWAYS love it. They have no needs, or their needs are magically met by whatever the man does, no matter how stupid, insensitive or violent. If he spends a lot of time in this activity, he is probably fantasizing that real women (like you) will act like his fantasy women and may have a hard time having a genuine sexual relationship where he has to actually deal with a real person who doesn't always act the way he wants.

Second, the vast majority of pornographic "relationships" show the man as the dominant person in the interaction. Some can be quite humiliating or even brutal toward the woman. Being really obsessed with this kind of porn may indicate a person who needs and wants to dominate you sexually and gets off on being in control of your body. You do NOT want this kind of person in your bedroom, not ever! A person who obsesses about violent or controlling sexual fantasies can be extremely dangerous to you later on.

If you can get a look at what he's so interested in, it could be very informative. A guy who is into looking at normal couples having sex might not be a big problem, depending how you personally feel about pornography. But someone who is into rape, or "barely legal" teens who look like they're 13, or bondage, or any kind of non-consensual or violent fantasies, is someone you don't want to be around.

Obession with Orgasm

Once you do become more sexual with a partner, Jerk signs become even easier to read. One "soft" sign is an obsession with orgasm, either yours or his. While worry about performance is not a rare affliction with normal men, an intense or obsessive need to "make you come" can be an indicator of a desire for control over your body. If this is present, look for other signs that go along with it – don't just assume it's because "men are like that." Some Jerks rely on sexual performance to help create the bond they need so that later on, when they start to become more abusive, their victim is hooked into the sexual satisfaction. Others just get a kick out of "making" you experience anything, because they feel in control that way. But if you end up feeling like he's forcing the issue when the chemistry isn't right, you will want to check for other Jerk indicators. If this happens with several other red flags, beware!

Pressuring You Sexually

The next level of Jerkiness would be to pressure you to do things that you don't want to do sexually. This can range from pressuring for intercourse when you're not ready for it, to insisting you perform oral or anal sex when you don't want to, or even asking you to participate in more extreme sexual behavior, such as "threesomes," partner swapping, bondage, or even rape fantasies.

> This was early in the relationship. I was about 45 years old at the time? I am now 50. He would say Strip! He would look at me with that smile and his eyes lit up. I just shook my head and looked away. He again said Strip! I wouldn't do it. I was pleading for him to stop. His dog began sobbing in the background!
>
> —Anonymous

> If I was sick or tired or just not in the mood, it didn't matter, he'd wake me in the middle of the night, masturbate against my naked body, insist on anal sex despite my protestations…
>
> —CH

Of course, if you personally want to engage in any particular kind of sexual activity that you enjoy, I am expressing no judgment here: please feel free to indulge in whatever turns you on. But if there's something you *don't* want to do and he tries to pressure, plead, guilt-trip, or even force you to do these things, you want to get away as fast as you can. This is particularly true for men who say, "You know you want it" or "Women always say 'no' when they mean 'yes,'" or "Women like (or need) to be dominated sexually." This kind of attitude is almost a 100% certain sign that you are going out with an abuser who will continue to escalate his demands until you are completely under his control. At the first sign of sexual pressure, let your partner know in no uncertain terms that this is not acceptable. If he continues, dump him. He is sure to be VERY big trouble the further you get into a relationship with him.

A part of this can be pressure to do things like his porno fantasy girls do. If he ever starts comparing you to a porno figure, or pressuring you to act in ways he's seen on pornographic videos, it's time to reconsider this relationship. He's seeing you as a fantasy, not a real person, and he wants you to be like those fantasy girls who would do whatever he wants and love it. You are not a fantasy sex toy – don't put up with that kind of thinking for one minute. If he can dehumanize you in that way, there's no telling how far he might go in his depraved fantasies.

> Pornography was a big issue, not at the beginning…but later, he would say I wasn't good enough, as I didn't do what "they" did, wasn't able to satisfy his needs, therefore he needed it. Later, we got the internet, and the pornography became a key role in his life.
>
> Most of the time it would be teenagers that he would watch on porn websites. I got to a point where he looked at teenagers walking down the street like he was undressing them with his eyes. This is where I got frightened for my daughters.
>
> −M, 37, 19-year abusive relationship

Abusive Jerks often talk about sex as a "need," especially as you get deeper into the relationship. He may feel that when he is sexually aroused or interested, you have an OBLIGATION to take care of his sexual needs, regardless of how you are feeling. He may also try to use sex as an indirect way to make up for him doing something mean or thoughtless, and get upset with you if you don't go along with his plan.

Any tendency to view sex as something you provide for him when he needs it is a very bad sign. This is particularly true if he makes veiled or even direct threats to seek sexual satisfaction somewhere else if you don't "put out" when he needs you to. That you are sick or have your period or just had a baby doesn't seem to be relevant information to such a man. He feels you are his possession and he has sexual "rights" that he may exercise any time he wants. This often becomes far worse if you are married, as now, in his mind, he has an official "title" to your body. So if you see any early signs of this attitude, stick to your boundaries and let him be upset. If he really does go elsewhere, you're going to be better off to be rid of him.

Promiscuity

It follows from the above that a lot of Jerks are promiscuous. For some reason, in our culture, women who sleep around a lot are considered "sluts" and are criticized for their loose morals, while men who sleep around a lot are considered "studs" and are admired for it. But it should be obvious that a guy who has a lot of female partners is going to be a bad risk. He most likely considers women to be interchangeable, and as romantic and sweet and genuine as he might seem, he's probably using a routine that he's used before on many other unsuspecting victims. You may be falling madly in love with him while he's calculating on his calendar how he can get in time with all three girlfriends this week without them finding out about each other.

> For my ex it was an obsession with sex and other women. Sexually he was never satisfied and told me that he went after other women purely for sex (lucky them). Whenever we had sex I knew that he would immediately want more and was made to feel this was yet another area in which I wasn't good enough for him. He used to hit on my friends until it got to the stage that I didn't tell him if they were coming to the house because he would deliberately wait in so that he could see them and leer at them.
>
> –TR, England, 25-year abusive relationship

Cheating on Another Partner

Similar warnings should apply to a married or committed person who would have a sexual relationship with you while still with his partner. This should be a no-brainer, but for some reason it isn't: if he'd cheat on his current partner, odds are phenomenal that he'll cheat on you, too. It's easy to go with the fantasy that his current partner "doesn't understand him" and that he's with you because he's "discovered true love" and has "realized what he was missing." But you can bet that before too long, he'll be sleeping with someone else complaining about how you don't understand him, either.

My recommendation is NEVER to go out with a person who is married or in a committed relationship, no matter what they say. If he is so dissatisfied with his relationship, tell him to go ahead and end it and then come back and tell you how it went. You'll be interested to hear about his experience, but you're NOT going out with him until he's clearly done with anyone else. Most of the time, he won't do it, because what he really wants is to have his cake and eat it, too. Again, you're just a convenience for him that he can dispose of anytime. Have the dignity not to allow yourself to play that role for anyone.

Sexual "Ownership"

Part of the belief that he "owns" you sexually is the belief that he can control what interactions you have with other men, or sometimes even women. This is often combined with an irrational jealousy that becomes more intense the more committed you become. In fact, this is one of the reasons abusers like to make those fast commitments we talked about in Chapter 5 – it allows them to establish their sexual "rights" over you early on.

This may start out as "jokes" or comments about other guys finding you hot, or asking you if someone "turns you on." These comments often seem or feel kind of odd – sort of unexpected, coming out of left field, as they say. Don't pass them off as oddities – take note and follow up. Find out what his attitude is toward you having contact with other people, especially other men. If he makes a "joke" about you wanting to have sex with someone you were only talking with, or with whom you've been friends for a long time, don't laugh it off. Ask him what he means by his comment. Ask him what he thinks about men and women having friendships that are non-sexual in nature. Ask him if it would bother him if you have male friends that you see without him being there. If he has any hesitation in supporting your right to hang out with anyone you want, of either gender, he is most likely a Jerk who thinks he owns you sexually once you're "his girlfriend."

Listen also for comments about other people. Does he often comment about couples that "they're probably sleeping together" or "she is totally hitting on him?" Does he make similar comments during movies or TV shows? Does he tend to interpret any male-female relationship as being sexualized? These are red flags that should send you looking deeper for his attitude toward relationships between the sexes. A feeling of sexual ownership in relationships means your partner views you as an object or possession that he has the right to control. The early signs may be subtle, but don't hesitate to look further if these comments happen frequently.

Contraception and Pregnancy

Finally, a very common area where attitudes of superiority and ownership come out strongly is around birth control. It is an interesting fact that many male Jerks somehow don't feel that birth control is their problem. After all, THEY aren't the ones getting pregnant! This is another one of those areas where social custom supports Jerky behavior and makes it seem like it's not so bad. But if you think about it, believing that birth control is solely your partner's concern is incredibly self-centered and irresponsible. And, as we have seen, self-centeredness and irresponsibility are the key underlying characteristics of a Jerk. So this area deserves very careful attention.

For starters, many Jerky guys won't use condoms. Of course, many have no problem with condoms and many non-Jerks don't like them particularly, but it's something to take note of. If they don't, ask them why not. Reasons may vary from "I can't feel anything" to "It takes the romance out of it" to "It just takes me out of the mood." Now, these may be perfectly legitimate reasons in themselves. But does your partner consider that YOU may not enjoy sex as much if you have to interrupt your activities to take care of birth control? Or that taking birth control pills may have adverse effects on your health? You're looking for that self-centered attitude that says, "My experience is more important than yours." Birth control should be a negotiated agreement where both partners come to some understanding of the needs of the other person. It requires some level of caring and sensitivity to work through this in a respectful way. Have that conversation and see how he handles it. If he's surprised that you bring it up, or simply leaves it up to you to take care of, that's a big red flag. If he thinks he can tell you what to do ("I think you should just take the Pill"), that's an even bigger one. Optimally, he should either bring it up himself or should be very interested in your feelings on the matter – after all, you are the one taking the risk of getting pregnant. If he doesn't consider that possibility to be his concern, he's not someone you want to be involved with.

> My husband didn't want to use condoms because "they're all too small for him" (OK, he's endowed, but not to that extreme!) and because they make it less sensitive.
>
> −CF, 35, Vermont, married 5 years

> He had no problem wearing a condom [the first time] as I insisted, but later made comments that I had them and he used the last one in the box. That was the last time he ever used one, too. After time went by he bragged more

and more about his abilities in bed, but what worried me the most was the way he HAD to be reassured by me. He would and still does to this day say things like "Tell me it's mine," "Tell me I'm the best you've ever been with"…etc. It was never "tell me 'you're' mine" but "it's."

—SG, 35, 1½-year abusive relationship

Also take note if they are willing to forge forward with sexual intercourse without any discussion of birth control having occurred. This is another common attitude that is supported in the media (how often do couples in the movies pause to discuss birth control options?) but should always be challenged. If he responds with, "I assumed you would take care of that," he believes birth control is your problem. While otherwise decent men can sometimes make this kind of inappropriate assumption, don't let them get away with it. Stop and have the discussion and make it clear that you believe it is as much his responsibility as yours to make sure no accidental babies occur. If he has a hard time with this concept, put your clothes back on and call a cab. He cares more about his own experience than whether or not you end up with a baby you had not planned to give birth to. And if he has the audacity to suggest that "it doesn't really matter, you can always have an abortion," I hope I don't have to tell you he's sure to be a Jerk Supreme.

Similarly, the danger of contracting sexually transmitted diseases is very real, and women are generally more vulnerable than men to this possibility. If you are not feeling comfortable having unprotected sex, he should not be, either. *Any* pressure for you to engage in unprotected sex when you've made your wishes clear should be an automatic deal-breaker. A person who is willing to give you an STD or AIDS or get you pregnant just because they'll enjoy the momentary sexual experience more is at best incredibly thoughtless, and may ultimately prove quite dangerous as well.

Even more evil is the concept of birth control sabotage. This is one that the media tend to associate more with women – claiming she is on the pill and "accidentally" getting pregnant so she can "snare" the man she wants. It may be hard to imagine, but I know of examples where men have done the same thing. My favorite one is claiming, "I'm sterile – I can't have children, the doctor told me so." You'd better get the medical records before you buy that one – I know of at least two cases personally where the woman ended up pregnant by a "sterile" man, who was in both cases just BAFFLED and very upset with those awful doctors for misleading them! Clearly, they lied about their supposed "sterility" so they could overcome their partner's objections and have unprotected sex without concern for the consequences. When you're pregnant is way too late to find out you've been lied to. So don't buy off on that idea. Seriously, check his medical records. If he objects, either he uses condoms or you dump him. You have a right to protect yourself from unwanted pregnancy, and it is by no means rude to set those kinds of expectations.

As you may recall, this is how Annie ended up pregnant. Larry told her he'd been exposed to radiation in the military, and became sterile. The doctors supposedly told him he couldn't have children, so therefore, birth control was not an issue. Annie was about 40 and had never wanted to have children, but she believed him, and a few months later found herself pregnant with his child and 3000 miles away from her home and support network.

Another more subtle form is when you've agreed to a particular form of birth control and he "can't wait" to employ it. He may have "forgotten" the condoms he promised to bring, or he may say he doesn't want to interrupt the moment, or he may confuse you about the time of your last menstrual cycle, and say, "It's safe now, you've already ovulated a week ago." Whatever the words, any effort to alter the agreed-upon birth control arrangements is an indication of self-centeredness that should never be ignored.

Check also if he has other babies that he's made but isn't caring for. The excuse in these cases is often, "She won't let me see the baby, because she's such a bitch," or, "Her family always hated me." Watch also for, "I don't pay child support because she never lets me see the baby." While there are situations where an angry ex-partner won't let the dad (or mom) see the kids, the odds are substantial that he's not seeing the kids either because he doesn't care about them, or because he's been awful to her or the kids and they're trying to protect themselves from his evil behavior. And if he has two or more kids by different moms and BOTH or ALL of them are so mean as to deprive him of contact, you know he's full of it, and is a high-powered Jerk for sure.

It is important to remember that abuse is about CONTROL, and one of the most effective ways to control a woman is to get her pregnant. The abusive Jerk can now pin you down to "exclusiveness" ("don't you want to be with the father of your own baby?"), can create economic dependency ("how will you support the baby without me?") and can control you by asserting his legal rights ("It's my baby, too, and I'll go for custody if you don't do what I want."). And that control starts with the sexual act. Effective birth control is a vitally important defense against losing control of your life. Anybody that would play around with the possibility of pregnancy, or worse, intentionally use it to trap you, is someone you want to stay very far away from.

SOME SIMPLE SCREENING TOOLS FOR SEXUAL JERKINESS

1) Set some sexual boundaries early in the relationship. Say goodbye at the door and see how he handles it. Delay getting "hot and heavy" for a while, until you're really comfortable with him and with your relationship. Let him know you want to get to know him as a person before moving to a more intense level of intimacy. If he resists this, pressures you to go farther, compares you to prior relationships, jokes about you being "old fashioned," accuses you of distrusting him, suggests he may go elsewhere for sexual satisfaction, or swears undying commitment to you if only you'll take him to bed, you're in with a manipulator who wants you only for what you can provide him sexually. Unless you're looking for trouble, let this one go quickly.

2) Listen carefully to conversations about sex and sexuality. How much is about the person he is with, and how much about his own performance? Does he boast about what he's able to "do to" a woman? Do his comments reflect an obsession with his own abilities or a need to impress you with his sexual prowess? He may not reveal this in conversations with you, but listen to his talk with his friends – is there a lot of male banter about conquests and sexual dominance? If you have any contact with a prior girlfriend, ask her about this area – How did he talk about sex? Was there give and take in the bedroom, or did he try to call all the shots? Again, this is one of the "soft" signs, but if you hear a tendency toward sexual egotism, screen carefully for other red flags, because a big ego in the bedroom often associates with a belief in his right to dominate you in other areas as well.

3) Find out his attitude toward pornography, by observation, from friends, or by directly asking him yourself. While this is definitely not a first date activity, if you are getting serious about someone, this is a good thing to know about. Be clear about your own feelings about this – for some women, use of porn is a deal-breaker, and he should know this if it is. But just as important, find out if he spends a lot of time and money in this area. Also find out what his preferences are, if you can. They will tell you a lot about him. If he's really into violent or degrading sexual fantasies, it doesn't bode well for his treatment of you.

4) Once you do get involved with him on a sexual basis, monitor very carefully for signs of a need to dominate you. Watch for behavior or comments that suggest that you need to take a passive role in sexual encounters, and that he calls the shots. If he wants to play out any fantasies, listen carefully for the content.

Anything that suggests that you "say no but mean yes" or "like to be dominated" are to be regarded as a very high danger sign. If you are hearing these signs, call a halt to any further sexual activity until you can have a serious talk about this. Let him know that you do not need to be dominated, that no means no, and that you do NOT appreciate him telling you or assuming what you like or prefer. If he in any way has a hard time with this, get rid of him immediately. He views you as a possession or object and will not respect that you are a separate individual, in the bedroom or out of it.

5) Check for orgasm obsession – yours or his. The very simple way to do this is to decide you're not in the mood to continue once or twice after he's getting warmed up and see how he reacts to this. "I'm kind of tired – I think I'd rather just take a bath and relax." A lot of Jerks can't handle this, either because they want to get what they want, or they're very invested in "making you come" so they can prove their prowess and dominance over you. Change the rules and assume some control of the situation and see how he reacts. A real man will be willing to roll with whatever you're up for – a Jerk won't let you have control. If he has to MAKE you have an orgasm, he's a control freak and likely to be a lot of trouble.

6) Be very clear and firm from day one about what you are and are not interested in doing sexually. If he pleads, pressures, or threatens to get you to do something you've said you don't enjoy, or if he just proceeds to do it without your consent, you're in with someone who gets a kick out of violating your boundaries. Taken to an extreme, this kind of person is a rapist. You don't want him in your bedroom. And any comparison with his "porn girls" is way out of line. You're not a fantasy – you're a person and have every right to assert your wishes in the bedroom, regardless of how he feels about it. If he can't agree to that, in actions as well as in words, you don't want him around.

Similarly, if he complains that you're not "ready" when he is, or implies that you must meet his sexual "needs" or he'll have to look elsewhere, you don't need to screen any further. You have a right to decide when you're in the mood or not, just as he does. You don't expect him to be ready on command when you're feeling hot, so why should he expect it of you?

A crafty way to get at this one is to ask him if he believes in the possibility of marital rape. Don't let him know what you think ahead of time – just ask him if he thinks a man can rape a woman if they're married. You could frame it as an argument you were having with a friend, and you'd like his judgment on it. If he says "no," I'd be done with him then and there. He thinks that marriage means you own your partner sexually and that she's there to service his sexual needs on demand. Unless you want to be a sexual slave, you don't need that kind of attitude in your household.

7) Be very aware of any signs of sexual ownership. This includes jealousy about other men (or sometimes even women), even if only in the form of "joking" comments about you sleeping with someone else or someone else "hitting" on you. Be really clear from the start that you will talk to anyone of either gender any time you please, and he can keep his comments about sleeping around to himself. If he can't trust you to talk to someone without going to bed with them, he's paranoid and obsessed in a very unhealthy way. Believe it or not, this kind of obsessiveness is associated with extreme violence and even murder in a more developed relationship. Most of the murder-suicides you read about in the paper are by obsessive guys who "loved" their partners so much they couldn't let anyone else have them. It's not something to take at all lightly.

8) Check for signs of promiscuity. Remember that an obsession with the possibility that YOU are sleeping around suggests that HE may be doing the same thing. Don't be paranoid, but don't ignore obvious signs, either. Short, stormy relationships are common for a certain kind of Jerk. Having more than one partner at the same time, including dating YOU while he's going out with someone else, is not something you want to accept. Check with prior partners and see if he has been unfaithful. If he has, he probably will be with you, too. And as I said above, if he's in a committed relationship, don't go near him until he's well clear of the former partner, including some time to recover from the loss. The ability to discard a former partner quickly and easily in exchange for a new one is not an admirable quality at all. It suggests shallowness and selfishness, which are earmarks of Jerky behavior.

9) Have a serious conversation about birth control well before you consider sleeping with him. See what kind of attitudes he has. Does he consider it your problem? Does he come "prepared," or does he just assume you are taking care of this without even asking you? Does he resist condoms or any form of self-restraint in this area because he finds it uncomfortable or inconvenient? Does he ask you your views or simply tell you how you should handle it?

Does he pressure you to have unprotected sex, because he'd prefer it that way? Or set up scenarios where passions are running high and birth control is not ready to hand? Does he dismiss the possibility of AIDS or other STDs out of hand, and leave you feeling silly or petty or insulting of him for bringing up the issue? Does he "forget" that he agreed to a certain plan, or try to convince you that you "misremembered" what you know you agreed to?

Any of these would be very serious concerns for me, because they show a disregard for the fact that you are the one who would carry this accidental baby if it occurred. But even more serious: does he pressure you to have a baby with him when you're not ready? Does he seem to want to have unprotected sex more urgently when you are likely to get pregnant? Does he have other babies that he's made which he doesn't take care of or "isn't allowed to see"? If any of these things are true, he's probably trying to get you knocked up to get more control over you, and if he's got other babies that he doesn't seem to care for, this won't be the first time he's done it. Any hint that this is going on should be enough for you to end the relationship on the spot.

Don't ever allow social myths and expectations to dictate your behavior in the sexual arena. Set your boundaries early and firmly, and send anyone who doesn't respect them packing ASAP. You are not a possession, and anybody who treats you that way is sure to be a Jerk with a capital "J". Saying "no" in the sexual arena is one of the surest ways to have a Jerk show his true colors before you're too deeply involved to escape from his control.

CHAPTER 13

Gut Feelings

IT WOULD BE QUITE POSSIBLE TO READ THIS WHOLE BOOK AND THINK, "Gosh, every man I know fits some of these characteristics. Is every one of them a Jerk? Do I have to settle for the "least Jerky" person I can find, or just live alone the rest of my life?

It is true that many people may show one or even several of the Jerk signs I have written about, and yet still be capable of a good relationship. And there are occasional Jerks who might not fit any of the indicators very clearly, and yet still be mean or even dangerous. So what's the final test if you've done the screening and are still not quite sure?

There is one screening method that I haven't mentioned, which is the simplest and most reliable method of all. And without this approach, the rest of these screening tools could just lead to more confusion. This method is called "trusting your gut."

Trusting your gut is NOT to be confused with "going with the flow" or "trusting your feelings." Quite the contrary – going with our feelings can be exactly what gets us into trouble in the first place. "He is so romantic, he makes me feel really good about myself, we're great in bed together, everyone thinks he's really handsome" – these are the phrases we use to talk ourselves into denying or explaining away the kind of gut feelings I am talking about. Going with your gut means being able to set aside your momentary feelings, wishes, fears, ambitions, and really take an honest look at the person in front of you.

Most every abuse survivor I have talked with has described more than one point early in their relationship where they had a feeling something wasn't quite right about this guy or how he related to them. They couldn't put their finger on exactly what, but there was a quiet voice inside them that said, "This guy is not for real." Some even paid attention to that "little voice" early on and tried to tell the person they weren't interested.

Annie, for instance, spent months dodging her eventual partner, telling him she didn't want to go out with him and politely declining all invitations. He arranged to meet her at various functions and worked on creating common ground, and asked her so many times to go out with him that she finally relented. A few months later, she was living 3000 miles away from her support system and pregnant with his child, and he began to show a very abusive side that had been carefully disguised while he was courting her. Needless to say, she wished she'd stuck with her initial assessment, as it took her several years and all of her family's support to completely extract herself from the situation.

Her initial red flag was pretty clear but might seem minor: he seemed to smoke a lot of marijuana. She had decided long ago that she would not go out with anyone who smoked marijuana, used drugs, or drank a lot, so he was off the list. Her gut told her that such people were a bad risk, and she'd clearly told him not to waste his time. Yet she went with him in the end. So where did she go wrong?

Somewhere along the line, she invalidated her own idea about what was a safe and healthy partner. She ignored her "gut feeling" that such a person would be a bad risk. She already knew on some level that she should not be involved with him, but she allowed his charm and persistence to convince her otherwise.

Jan, on the other hand, trusted her instincts and observations. She was willing to go along with the romance, but did notice her beau asking for receipts after each of their romantic meals. This struck her as odd, and she made a note of it. When things started to get uncomfortable, she went ahead and asked him why he did it, and found out he'd been taking their romantic dinners off on his taxes. She also noticed his willingness to take advantage of teenagers to illegally fund his college education, and seeming lack of remorse for doing so, as well as his tendency to want her to do things he knew she didn't like just to keep him happy. Within a couple of months, she decided he wasn't worth her time.

The "Little Voice"

As you read through this book, you may come across a range of behavior that your newest paramour may be displaying. How do you move from there to deciding if he's in or out for future dates?

The answer is to consult your gut level assessment skills. We all have them. It's that "little voice" that we all sometimes ignore but that later proves unerringly correct. At some point, when you've asked all the questions you can think of and checked out his history and talked to former girlfriends and consulted with your own friends and relatives, you have to make the final call. And that little voice is the one you want to learn to consult for that final decision.

You may remember me mentioning that checking with a younger child is a good screening tool. This works because most little kids haven't learned yet to distrust their own inner sense of what is safe or right. The average five-year-old can tell you in about two minutes whether someone seems nice or mean, regardless of any social tricks or charm they may display. It is only through years of adults telling us to believe things we know aren't true, being forced to comply with the demands of teachers, doctors, pastors, etc., whom we don't really trust, being told to do things that are "good for us" that we know to be a waste of time or dangerous, and seeing and hearing lots of stories about magical romances where loving women magically transform beasts into princes, that we learn slowly not to believe ourselves.

So we need to get back to that childlike direct knowledge, where we look at a situation and stop explaining to ourselves why it's OK. We need to set aside all fears, social ambitions, myths, stereotypes, and personal preferences, and really ask the hard question: what is this person really about?

There are some definite indications you can look for that tell you when you are paying attention to this inner sense and when you are working hard to ignore it. The first thing to know is that your "inner voice" generally doesn't press you with overwhelming emotion. That's why I refer to it as the "little voice" – it is often quiet and is easily drowned out with other social chatter. This voice is distinguished less by power than by persistence – it can even have a nagging, at times almost annoying quality about it, like a little child who won't leave you alone and wants your attention. It is easy to ignore in the short run but it keeps coming back to you, always present at some level, trying to communicate what you need to know.

> He called me from downtown, where he was bar hopping with his best friend. It didn't feel "right" to me. I couldn't handle being in a relationship with a man who still, at age 58, scoured the bars and called me from a dance club. I knew it was wrong for me. After I hung up the phone, I sent him an email and ended it, citing that while I meant no judgment against him, I just could not be in a relationship with someone who had that kind of lifestyle…. He "talked me out of it" big time, by saying that I was misjudging him, it was me he wanted to dance with, what kind of creep did I think he was. As it turned out, I was right – he was an alcoholic, lecherous, parasitic creep.
>
> **–TK, 59, Canada, abused 10 years**

You may be so used to ignoring this voice in the back of your mind that you have a hard time even hearing it anymore. But it's been there all along and its advice is usually right on. It's just that we've almost all gotten in the habit of telling ourselves not to listen.

Think back to a time you did something you knew was foolish or dangerous. Probably when you were a child or a teenager, you did something you knew was wrong. Maybe you stole money from your parents, or took something from a sibling, or drank or smoked or used drugs for the first time. Or maybe it was something where you went along with someone else to protect yourself – you went ahead and laughed at the kid being picked on even though you felt bad for him, or you left when you saw someone being hit or bullied. Maybe you even allowed an adult to do something abusive to you because you were afraid or didn't want to upset the adult or weren't sure anyone would believe you if you told them. Think of such a case and ask yourself – wasn't there a moment during that experience where you KNEW that what was happening wasn't right? No matter how you explained it to yourself during or after the event, wasn't there a part of you saying you should put down the drink, or say something to the bully, or tell the adult to stop? That is the voice we are talking about – that inner sense of right and wrong. You have it, I have it – everyone has it in them somewhere, but most of us have learned not to listen.

Overriding the Inner Voice

I am a person who hates to waste things. This applies particularly to food. I pride myself on shopping efficiently and on buying enough perishables to last the week with a minimum of spoilage. My kids will also tell you that I have an "iron stomach" and can eat things that no one else would touch. But sometimes I have ignored my own better judgment in the service of trying to prove my skills.

Very recently, I had splurged on some quality chicken at a higher-than-usual price. I had cooked it once and saved the rest for sandwiches. After a few days, I saw the chicken was still there and decided I'd better use it up before it went bad. As I took it out, I already was wondering whether it was too late based on the time that had gone by. This was the first sign of "the voice" talking to me. But I wanted it to still be good, because I couldn't stand the thought of throwing it away when it cost so much. So I thought I'd check by smelling it. I sniffed, and it wasn't obviously bad, but again, there was just a whiff of something less than savory. Still, I didn't want to believe it. "It should still be good," I told myself. "It's only been three days – it can't have gone bad yet. Besides, I spent a bunch of money on that – I want to get my money's worth." So I decided to make a sandwich and then get rid of the rest if I didn't like it. I did make the sandwich and I ate it, despite constant if quiet misgivings from "the voice," checking almost every bite for any sign of bad taste or decay. I finished the sandwich without noticing anything that seemed negative, though it certainly wasn't the best I'd ever tasted. But I immediately had a small but definitely bad feeling in my stomach, which I tried to deny existed.

I decided after I was done that no one else but me would even consider eating this and tossed the remainder of the chicken. The next day, I had low-level intestinal distress for most of the day, to the point that I had to stay home from work. I never threw up or got feverish, but I was definitely dancing on the edge of food poisoning.

So what happened? My "gut level" assessment (literally) was that the stuff was probably bad. No obvious signs, but enough subtle indications that it wasn't worth risking eating it. But social controls started to enter in. I didn't want to throw it out. It had cost a lot of money and I didn't want to feel I had wasted it. I hated the idea that I'd misjudged how long it would be good or bought more than we could eat. I did check for signs of spoilage, but I wasn't objective at all – I WANTED it to still be good because it would make me feel more competent and I could avoid the disappointment of knowing I'd spent extra money and wasted it. So I talked myself into believing it would be OK, even though I knew it really wasn't. It's not like I'm so poor I couldn't have tolerated the loss – it was my ego, my need to be RIGHT that kept me eating that bad sandwich, ignoring both mental and physical indications that I'd be better off tossing it in the garbage and making a new lunch.

While this was not a life-shattering event, it shows the process by which I got good information from my intuitive side, and then promptly used social explanations and justifications to keep from acting on it. If you are very honest with yourself, you will be able to find dozens or even hundreds of examples where you deny your gut feelings in favor of doing what is socially acceptable. Sometimes it is quite conscious – you may know your boss is a mean-spirited, power-hungry jackass, but you may still choose to laugh at his jokes because you don't want to get fired. But other times, it's kind of automatic – maybe you visit your mom and she says something that your gut tells you is a put-down, but you have schooled yourself to explain it away. "She's just like that." "She loves me, she just doesn't know how to express it." "I'm probably overreacting – I'm sure she didn't mean it that way."

Take a hard look at your own behavior, and see if you can identify where you've listened to that "little voice" and had good results, or where you've chronically ignored it and suffered as a result. You will see that the voice is there and available for consultation, but you probably have come up with some really good ways to tell it to be quiet.

Learning to Trust the Inner Voice

So how does this apply to Jerk screening? It's quite simple, actually, although it requires a willingness to be very honest with yourself. If you can notice the kind of things you say to talk yourself out of listening to that gut feeling, you'll be well on your way to identifying what it is you're trying to talk yourself out of, and maybe save yourself from something a lot worse than a day-long stomach ache.

> He was visiting a friend. So I was listening to music waiting for him. I felt so happy, and in love with him. S came back, and hugged me etc. asked me what I had been up to while he was gone. I said "nothing really," just out of habit. He just

screamed at me, "What the f*** do you mean nothing?" I was gobsmacked. It was the first time he ever talked to me like that. I instantly cried my eyes out. He then shouted "How can you do nothing for a couple of hours?! I'm going, we're over!" I begged for him to stay. He went out the door for like a minute, then came back. I asked him what was wrong. He said, "I really missed you, was looking forward to coming back to see you. I ask you what you've been up to, and you just say nothing really." I was soooo confused. I was so desperate for him not to leave me. I told him I'm sorry. Begged him to never say he's leaving me like that again, 'cause I just couldn't handle that. He forgave me, hugged me, and wiped my tears. He told me he loves me, and is staying forever....

From then on, this is one of his very favourite ways to upset me. That little voice told me "what a Jerk!" But when he comforted me, and told me I should've gave him a better answer, I talked myself out of it. "He was really looking forward to coming back to see me. I didn't answer very well. Should have just told him I'd been listening to music, and thinking about him," etc. He wasn't a Jerk anymore, and I was.

–JD

So you find yourself reflecting on your first date. You are feeling emotionally very good – kind of heady, a little out of control, perhaps. Maybe you've had a drink or two, maybe the night ended off with a nice "good night" kiss, maybe you're thinking all went pretty well. But you have a thought – wasn't the limousine rental a little expensive? Quickly, you tell yourself, "Well, he's got lots of money, it's not such a great expense for him." And you think, "He was pressuring to get me to invite him in, wasn't he?" But you explain to yourself, "Men are just like that – they get some of those male hormones going, they can't help themselves. Besides, he obviously is attracted to me or he wouldn't be pursuing me this way. I'm sure it's OK."

I hope you can hear some parallels with my story. "It's only been a few days – I'm sure the chicken can't be bad yet. Besides, it doesn't smell bad – it'll be OK. I'll be able to tell if I eat a bite..." It is that second voice, the one with all the easy explanations, that you have to watch out for. It tends to be loud enough to drown out your first intuitive impulse, and it tends to say things that you want to hear. This voice has no problem explaining why you shouldn't listen to that other voice – there is a perfectly logical explanation for everything that fits in with what you want to believe.

The moment you hear yourself doing this, STOP! There is something that you noticed that bothered you, or you wouldn't be working to explain why it is OK. Take a step back and look at what that item is that bothered you, and make a note of it. Maybe a limo isn't out of line for his income level, but your initial take was that it seemed over the top. Maybe a lot of men are naturally pushy in the area of sexuality, but you felt your boundaries being disrespected. That doesn't mean he's a loser, but don't talk yourself out of your observation. Just let it be there and make sure you've noticed and acknowledged your gut-level impulse (like Jan did about the dinner receipts). That way, you'll be a little more watchful the next time out for similar trends, and can maybe do a little further testing in the area.

> I believe it was our second or third date and he was first late (like a half hour at least) meeting me, and then his excuse was that he was having lunch with one of his friends. I thought, "Wow how inconsiderate of him! But oh, it happens, it's no big deal." Then he told me right after that that his friend was tagging along to the movie. I was upset, like "wtf?" But again, "Oh, he wants his friend to meet me. I shouldn't be mad at him," though I thought again how inconsiderate not to tell me beforehand. I felt like I was put on the spot after waiting for him while he was out having lunch with his friend.
>
> **–SA**

Explaining Away Your Gut

Here are some common sentences we use to talk ourselves out of our gut feelings:

"I'm sure he didn't mean it."

"You shouldn't think that way about people."

"You know how men are."

"It must be because he really likes me." ("It must be…" usually means you're justifying.)

"You're being overly sensitive."

"It's just a little quirk (bad habit, whatever)."

"After all, he's been through a lot." ("After all" is also a sign that you're explaining away your gut.)

"He's just trying a little too hard."

"You really need to give him a chance."

There are many more, and each of us has our favorites. But I want you to notice that what these sentences have in common is that they attempt to explain something. They encourage you to "be reasonable" or to "see the other side." These are the efforts of your conscious, social mind to keep your "little voice" from undermining the image that you want to create for yourself. You want to believe that it was a good date – you felt good, he seemed nice enough, you're lonely and you'd really like to have a boyfriend – why can't this be the right one? A part of you wants to stop analyzing and just "go with the flow" – to look at the good parts and hope the rest works out OK. It's totally normal to feel this way. It's very exciting to be dating someone new, and there's nothing wrong with trying to take an optimistic view. But take note of these quiet objections from your gut and remember them for later reference as you learn more about your potential partner. This information may mean very little, but it could also save you from a big mistake. Any time you find yourself explaining away a partner or potential partner's behavior, it's time to be more careful and analytical in your approach.

This can also work the other way – you can be overly paranoid and fearful, and you can just as easily ignore gut feelings and still end up in trouble. This sounds a little different – it's more like, "What do you expect from a man?" or "They're all like that" or "Do you really think someone like you can expect a lot better?" You may have learned to have a low opinion of men or of yourself early in life, maybe because you were abused yourself or exposed to abusive men in your environment. You may think it's pretty normal for men to be Jerky and thereby miss someone that could be great for you. In this case, your gut may be telling you that someone's very nice, but you tell yourself, "He just seems like that – they all turn into Jerks in the end," or "Why would he be interested in someone like me?" You may even think of this as an effective screening tool – expecting everyone to be a Jerk so you're not surprised. But in reality, you're denying your gut feelings just as much as your overly romantic sisters. Not all men are Jerks, and if you believe you deserve better, you just might find it. One reason you keep meeting Jerks may be that you don't think any normal person would like you.

> I was bridesmaid and him best man at a very small wedding, only 4 of us. Instantly I disliked him because he tried to crack on to me and then get me drunk. I didn't like that and we had words, we argued most of the night, I didn't like him. I drank enough my defenses were down and we ended up sleeping together, then I was gone.
>
> My thinking, I was 20, no real boyfriend ever, and he wanted me, so what ever he dished out in those early days I found an excuse for.
>
> I SHOULD HAVE LISTENED TO MY GUT!!!!!!!!!!!!!!!!!
>
> —AS, 56, Australia, 13-year abusive marriage

I worked with a woman once whose children were in foster care because of her drug use and various abusive boyfriends. Her mom was an alcoholic, her dad was abusive to them both, and all the men in her life, including the two fathers of her children, had been extremely abusive Jerks. She was asked out by someone who seemed very nice, but she told her therapist he was "too normal" for her. Her therapist replied, "Why don't you try 'normal' out – maybe you'll like it!" So she did. She actually broke up with him at one point because she couldn't handle the "normalcy" of it all, but he hung in there and they got back together and eventually got married and are doing really well. She got all but one of her kids back and hasn't been back in the system again, all because she challenged her assumptions and decided that her usual "type" might not really be what she needed.

So if your gut tells you someone seems nice, and you hear yourself saying things like, "But he seems so boring!" or "I really prefer the 'bad boy' type" or "He's probably a wimp," stop yourself again and see if you aren't silencing that small voice saying, "That guy will probably take care of me and I'm not sure I can handle it." Sometimes it's easier to stop hoping for what you really need than it is to take the risk on someone different than what you're used to.

The Gut Check

The other thing that can tell us whether you're in tune with your "gut" is your emotions. A true gut feeling is actually very stable. It's a truth that you know without always knowing exactly why, but it keeps coming back despite emotional noise that may distract away from it.

So a true gut feeling doesn't create confusion – it cuts through it to the core of what's really going on. If you are feeling anxious, proud, hopeful, resentful, hopeless – none of these feelings indicate a connection with the intuitive gut-level truth I'm talking about. Trusting your gut may be associated with a certain amount of fear, if it tells you to act in opposition to what is socially expected, and you know there may be adverse consequences. Or it may be accompanied by a kind of righteous anger, for example, if you are mustering the courage to challenge someone who is bullying you or others and you are preparing to face them down. But it will be a very simple kind of conflict – "I know Mary will be mad at me, but I have to do this, no matter what." Or, "I am not going to put up with this anymore, and I'm ready to fight you if necessary." There aren't a lot of "what-ifs" or "maybe I shoulds" associated with the gut-level truth. It just is what it is.

So the real trick here is to listen through all the what-ifs and maybes and to hear what you KNOW but perhaps don't want to believe. Sometimes what it requires is for you to stop all the social machinery going on in your head for a moment and just ask a very basic question.

For instance, if you end up your first date with your head in a whirl, feeling excited, hopeful, anxious, and maybe a bit confused, it may be time to take a deep breath and *think* for a moment instead of feeling. If you find yourself running through a lot of scenarios in your head, such as, "I think he's the one!" or "I've never met anyone so perfect!" or "I wonder if he really likes me?" it is time to stop for a moment and gain some perspective. Instead of asking how you feel about him, or what you believe about him, ask yourself what you KNOW about him. What has he shared with you? Did he seem like he was putting on a show, a bit over the top? Was he making all the decisions? Were you confused or hurt at any time? Did he treat others well? Did he seem genuine? Did he press you or test your boundaries in any way? Did he seem to get too close too quickly? In short, ask yourself the kind of questions I've outlined in this book.

> The first time bells started ringing for me was a walk we went on and we were having a chat, and although I don't remember exactly what was spoken about, I do remember clearly thinking that it was the oddest conversation I had ever had with someone. It was like he misunderstood everything I had said and then twisted it all to really get at me when all I had tried to do was

be myself and be positive. I often think back now to that walk as I know now I would walk the other way if I ever encountered someone like that again who made me feel all wrong when I had not done or said anything bad.

–FS

And then ask yourself one final question: Who is this guy? Gut level, no analysis, who is he? What is important to him, what does he want, what is he avoiding, what is he doing here on this earth? This is not a question about how you feel or what you want – it's about *his* motivations.

If your gut is telling you he's OK, carry on, but be prepared to do this again periodically. If there are any gut-level doubts, get more serious about figuring out what he's up to. Get back to Chapter 1 and start reading again, and check him out ruthlessly. That gut feeling is rarely completely off – it may not tell you what exactly is wrong, but if it's saying to watch out, you should listen.

And if you can't answer those questions at all – slow down. You don't know him well enough yet to let yourself fall. Most Jerks are experts at creating a very "soft" image of themselves, something they or you can modify to make into what you want it to be. They won't reveal a lot about who they are, because they want to leave the freedom to "edit" their personality to meet your needs. So very often, the very smooth Jerk will leave a general feeling that he's attentive and kind, but very little sense of who he really is. The inability to get a gut response after being with someone for a few hours is probably almost as concerning as getting a negative vibe.

Everyone has his/her own way of doing this "gut check." If my suggestions don't work, find your own way to do it. But be sure to do it. It's really about being honest with yourself about what's going on, about setting aside the romantic mythology, if only for a moment, and remembering that this is a real person, and real people can seem nice but actually be very mean.

> Of the many situations where I ignored my gut, I recall one where he asked me to give him money for a deposit of a house we rented together. And he suddenly wanted my part all cash, and I already knew if I would want it back he wouldn't give it back. That second I heard a voice in my head that just screamed: don't give him this money, use it to go away.
>
> I ignored it.
>
> —Anonymous, 24, Germany, abused 8 months

When it comes right down to it, the bulk of the Jerk's efforts are aimed at overwhelming or undermining this very ability to tell truth from falsehood, to tell good motivations from bad. They work very hard from the moment they meet you to put you off your guard, to assure you that they are the nicest possible people, that they'll put you on a pedestal and worship you, and that you have nothing to fear from them. Resisting those efforts, cultivating your gut intuition and trusting it, is the most important thing you can do to protect yourself from a Jerk, even if you forget everything else in this book. It can be very tough – we all want to believe that someone's going to come along and make things better for us, and Jerks are experts at playing on those desires. But on some level, you will be able to sense the game, and the more you practice at it, the better you will get. Take that "little voice" that speaks the truth, and make it just a little louder, and your Jerk Radar will be able to tell you when you're with a Jerk with almost 100% accuracy.

SOME TIPS ON TRUSTING YOUR GUT

1) Start by familiarizing yourself with your gut intuition in situations where there is less emotion involved. Remember my example with the bad chicken? You will have some areas where you want to believe the truth of something even when the facts contradict you. Maybe it's your tennis game (you like to believe you can beat someone that you can't) or betting (you KNOW you can pick the right numbers, even when you know the odds against it) or perhaps finding directions (I don't need the map – I know how to get there, and I sure am not asking for directions!). See how you talk yourself out of what you know. Listen to the sentences in your head. Write some of them down and then see where else you use them. Sort out the ones that are anxious or ambitious or that are driven by social pressures from the ones that are internal and solid and reliable. The more you notice these tendencies in low-risk situations, the easier it will be to recognize them when the stakes are high.

2) Notice also the emotions you experience when you go with your gut, and when you don't. Be aware of the extra anxiety, uncertainty or confusion that happens when you are getting away from where your instincts tell you to go. Work is usually an easy place to do this – there are often situations where you feel you need to act a certain way to do your job properly, or maintain office relations, or keep your boss from getting upset. Compare this to when you really speak your mind and see the difference between the two. A good relationship should allow you to get closer to expressing those gut level truths aloud.

Family can also be a place to study this, if you can muster the proper perspective. After all, it's most likely in your family that you learned the social rules that often overrule your gut instincts. Take a good look at who has to defer to whom, at who has control, and at what role you play. Notice what happens when you "go along to get along" and when you let people know what is true for you even when they don't want to hear it. Notice how they react, and notice how you feel. Do others resist you speaking your mind? Do you get shouted down? Met with cold silence? Do you feel strong? Weak? Anxious? Hopeful? Which of these are associated with you being honest with yourself? Which are associated with talking yourself into things you don't really believe?

3) Once you are comfortable recognizing your gut reactions to things, as well as how you can talk yourself out of them, observe yourself before, during and after contact with your partner or potential partner. Do you find yourself doing things to convince HIM that YOU are OK? Are you changing yourself to make him like you? Of course, everyone does this to some degree, especially early in a relationship. But if you find yourself doing a lot of accommodating, go back and do the "gut check" – what is this guy really about? What are his motivations? What has he shared about himself? Do you even have a clue who he is?

4) Once you've done your initial "gut check," review any behavior that he may have engaged in that made you wonder. Don't speculate – just ask yourself directly – "Was he trying to get me to sleep with him?" "Did he just say that because he thought I'd like it?" "What do his comments about his ex tell me about his view of women?" Ask these as dispassionately as possible – you don't want a particular response, you just want to be open to hearing the answer.

5) Most importantly, ask yourself whether he's said or done anything that you felt uncomfortable about, even for a moment. Check your internal sentences – are you explaining his behavior for him? Are you creating justifications or explanations for something you didn't understand or didn't like? Are you telling yourself that you're being too sensitive or that you're being unreasonable? Did he himself *suggest* that you were being too sensitive? Did HE say any of those things you are now saying to yourself in your head?

These attempts to explain away odd or uncomfortable behavior are almost always efforts to submerge your gut instincts in favor of some hopeful scenario you don't want to let go of. If you hear them, STOP! Back up and look again at the behavior. Yes, he did brush against your breast with his hand, and no, it probably was not accidental. Yes, that gleam in his eye when he looked at you WAS a little creepy. Yes, he did look like he was laughing inside when you shared your musical preferences, even though he claimed he agreed with you. Yes, he was driving too fast on the freeway and seemed generally impatient. No, you didn't imagine that he changed the topic every time you asked him about his past relationships – he really did. Don't try to explain them – just validate your observations and stop trying to explain them away. Then make a plan to check further into these areas, instead of just hoping you were wrong or pretending it will go away.

6) Do the "Girlfriend check:" if your girlfriend told you about the things this guy is doing with you, would it bother you in any way? It's often easier to see things more clearly when someone else's relationship is involved. This can be a great way to check your gut when emotions are running high – if it's not OK for your girlfriend, why would it be OK for you?

7) If you do find your gut telling you something is wrong or something needs to be said, SAY IT. Don't worry that you'll offend him – remember, if he's a Jerk, you WANT to challenge him and see how he handles it. A real man will listen and try to understand what you're saying. A Jerk will either work to explain to you why your perceptions are wrong, or get upset with you. The super smooth ones will make it seem like they're listening ("I can really understand how you could feel that way") but will still somehow manage to convince you that you are wrong. If you're dealing with a person who is really trying, you should come away from this conversation feeling like you understand them better, either reassured that you may have made some incorrect assumptions, or with some food for thought on how this relationship is likely to proceed. But with a Jerk, you may very well feel a little confused, a little defeated, and perhaps doubting your original perceptions without having received a really valid explanation. In short, your gut will still be telling you that you're being duped, even if his explanation sounded totally reasonable. It's very important to notice this feeling AFTER a confrontation. Caring confrontation should lead to better mutual understanding. If it leads to further confusion, you're almost surely dealing with a Jerk who is working to convince you that what you see isn't true.

When it comes right down to it, the best screening for a Jerk is being yourself, and not worrying about trying to please your partner too much. Of course, you want to be polite and respectful, but never at the cost of your own integrity. It feels GOOD to stick up for yourself, even if your date is surprised or offended by your behavior. If your gut is telling you to say something, speak up. If your gut is telling you it's time to leave, then make your departure. If it's saying not to let him in the house, don't let him in. And if he has trouble with that, if he's upset about it, if he decides not to go out with you because of it – GOOD! You have screened out someone who would have been a lot of trouble and could even have been very dangerous.

Despite what the fairy tales and romantic movies tell us, you don't need a man to be happy or safe. The best way to accomplish both happiness and safety is to be yourself and to do what you believe is right, and let the Jerks "reject" you if they don't like it. The very best Jerk Radar skill is just that – let them think or feel whatever they want. If they don't like you just the way you are, they can look somewhere else for a more willing victim. If you're a naturally helpful person, be helpful – but don't let someone play on your helpfulness in order to get control of you. It's OK to say NO, it's OK to follow your own path, and a person who really cares about you will support you in doing what feels right to you.

Any time you feel your gut intuition violated, speak up and let your truth be known. You'll know who you are dealing with by their reactions. If they don't like you speaking up, you're better off on your own. If you really believe that, and act on it, the Jerks will see it and run the other way. And you may soon find yourself meeting a different kind of person, the kind who wouldn't have approached you before, a kind you may not even have been interested in, but who really appreciate your directness and integrity. That's the kind of person with whom a real relationship can be built. It may not be as exciting and romantic as in the movies, but in the long run, excitement and romance are overrated. A real relationship is built on trust and honesty.

Be yourself and trust that gut feeling. Anyone who doesn't like you for who you are, you are better off without. Once you realize that you don't NEED any particular man to make you feel OK, your Jerk Radar will kick into high gear. The men you meet will no longer see a passive princess ready to be rescued. They'll see a smart, savvy, no-nonsense woman who knows what she wants and isn't afraid to insist on it. And the Jerks will run for the exits!

The Jerk Radar Quiz

S O THERE YOU HAVE IT. YOU CAN NOW SEE HOW YOU HAVE BEEN PRO-grammed to be vulnerable to a Jerk's charms. You have learned the kind of tactics to expect from a Jerk and how to figure out what their real motivations might be. And you've learned a few tests you can run if you're not quite certain if you've got a Jerk on your hands or not. Now it's time to put it all together with the Jerk Radar Quiz!

If you are still uncertain, this Quiz should be a big help, because it looks at all the Jerky behaviors across the spectrum. A person may have a big ego and be OK in other areas, or have some old-fashioned ideas about gender roles but be otherwise respectful and kind. But the true Jerk will score at least moderately high in multiple areas. While he or you may be able to explain away a particular area, a high score on the Quiz will tell you that those explanations don't hold much water.

This is not a scientific test. It's more along the lines of a screening tool. It should give you a general idea of how your current partner measures up against the Jerk Radar tests I've outlined in the book. That being said, I have field tested this quiz with the members of the online survivor community who shared most of the stories you've been reading. The lowest score their Jerky partners had was 26, and the highest was over 50. When they applied this same quiz to "normal" guys they had dated before or after their primary Jerk, the highest score was 8. So I think it's a pretty good tool to distinguish Jerks from decent guys.

Remember that Jerkiness occurs along a spectrum – there is no black and white line where you can say anyone above this point is a Jerk, and those below are not. But a high Jerk score will definitely indicate that you should take a closer look, and a really high score will strongly suggest that you seek greener pastures. The higher the score, the more quickly you should run!

This quiz has 50 questions. Most are yes/no questions, and your date scores one point for a "yes" answer and zero for a "no." There are some (such as whether he has prior criminal acts) where he will score one point for each instance. And some things (like having an affair with you while in a committed relationship to someone else) get more than one point because they're stronger indicators of trouble.

Add up the score for each section, and then add them all together for a final score at the bottom. The meaning of the scores will be explained at the end.

Jerk Radar Quiz

(Score one point for each "yes" answer. If unsure, go with your gut!)

1) Excessive Charm
    a) Does he spend more money than would seem normal on you, especially early in your relationship?
    b) Does he shower you with flattering remarks, about your looks, intelligence, abilities, style, or anything that seems beyond expectations?
    c) Does he ask a lot of questions about you but seem reluctant to talk about his own experience or opinions until you've told him about yours?
    d) Does he seem to agree with you about all of your tastes, preferences and opinions?
    e) Does he surprise you with complex, expensive or elaborate plans that you are expected to go along with every time?

    SCORE:_____

2) Big Ego
    a) Does he focus a lot on "always looking his best?" Or, does he give lots of advice on how you should dress or what you say in public gatherings?
    b) Does he often speed or drive unsafely or get excessively upset about having to wait in traffic?
    c) Does he boast or name-drop in order to appear important?
    d) Is he overly competitive in conversations or games or sports?
    e) Does he brag or boast about how good YOU look to his friends – as if your appearance is somehow his accomplishment?

    SCORE:_____

3) Isolation/Intensity
   a) Does he want you to spend most of your time with him, or do you find yourself spending most of your time with him and neglecting other activities or people you used to value?
   b) Does he say he loves you, that you're "the one," or talk about long-term commitment (e.g., being "exclusive," moving in, moving away, getting married, or having kids) within a very short a period of starting to date?
   c) Does he make subtle or not-so-subtle comments downgrading some of your friends or family, or accusing them of not liking him or "not being supportive" of your relationship with him?
   d) Does he pressure you to change your plans or go along with his, even if you don't want to? (Score 2 if there is pressure to be involved sexually too quickly or in ways you are not comfortable with, including discouraging birth control.)
   e) Is he unreasonably jealous or suspicious about your contacts with other friends or family (especially with other men)?

   SCORE:_____

4) Irresponsible/Lazy
   a) Does he have a hard time admitting he is wrong? Does he blame others for his errors, make excuses for them, or minimize their significance?
   b) Does he have a spotty job history?
   c) Do you often find that you have "misunderstandings" in which somehow you are always the one who misunderstood him?
   d) Does he avoid unpleasant tasks or procrastinate to excess?
   e) Does he gamble excessively or have large debts?

   SCORE:_____

5) Clingy/Dependent
   a) Does your partner focus on telling stories about his difficult past, and stress how important you are for him to overcome it?
   b) Does he ever say things like "I couldn't make it without you" or "you are my life" or "you are the only one that can ever help me"?
   c) Does he become moody, depressed or irritable when he does not get his way?
   d) Do you ever find yourself changing plans or canceling activities because he "needs you right now"?
   e) Does he become upset, or do you end up feeling guilty, when you take time to be alone or engage in activities without him present?

   SCORE: _____

6) Attitude Toward Women
   a) Does he put down or consistently criticize and blame his ex-partner(s) for past bad relationships?
   b) Does he enjoy or make demeaning jokes or comments about women or other low-status groups in society?
   c) Does he tell you that men and women have very different roles in society, or get upset when you challenge or disagree with his views on gender roles?
   d) Does he treat other women or people he believes are "below him" in social status as servants or with disrespect?
   e) Does he put you or other women on a pedestal, grouping certain women into near goddesses and comparing you or them to the group of "bad women" (feminists, female bosses, ex-partners, prostitutes, loose women, or any such grouping) whom he disrespects and criticizes?

   SCORE: _____

7) Who Makes the Rules?
   a) Do you find your recollections called into question when you know for sure what you and he have agreed to? Do you find yourself doubting your own recollections when he says you remembered wrong?
   b) Does he use guilt trips or emotional pressure to get you to change your plans?
   c) Does he object to you doing things that he thinks are OK for him (such as hanging out or flirting with the opposite sex)?
   d) Does he expect you to clean up after him or do other menial tasks that he feels are beneath him?
   e) Does he react negatively (by denial or by attacking you) when confronted about double standards or when you stick to your boundaries or plans?

   SCORE: _____

8) History of Abuse
   a) Does he have a history of interpersonal criminal behavior (assault, rape, child abuse, armed robbery)? (Score one point for each instance of known criminal behavior, even if he was not convicted.)
   b) Does he have any past restraining orders, no-contact orders, child abuse allegations, or supervised visitation orders with his children? (Score one point for each area that applies.)
   c) Has he lied about or failed to reveal any behavior or situation identified in question 7a or 7b?
   d) Does he have a reputation for (or admit to) a temper or "anger problems"?
   e) Does he have a history of tumultuous relationships, with

sudden endings and bad feelings and drama, or multiple separations and reunions with the same partner?

SCORE: _____

9) Addictive Behavior
   a) Does he drink to excess more than once or twice a year (score 1)? Does he drink more than 1–2 drinks every day (score 1)? Does he use any illegal drugs (score 1 for marijuana, 2 for anything more serious – includes using any prescription drug in ways other than prescribed)
   b) Does he gamble, use porn, or engage in any other indulgent behavior to excess?
   c) Does he use drinking, drugs or any other compulsion to explain away negative behavior?
   d) Has the person accrued any negative consequences for his addiction (excessive bills, loss of jobs, loss of relationships, loss of driver's license, criminal charges) without any big changes in the behavior?
   e) Does he try to involve you in his addictive behavior (encouraging drinking, wanting to watch or act out porn scenes with you when you're not interested, wanting to take you gambling even though you don't like it)?

SCORE: _____

10) Sexual Obsession/Manipulation
   a) Does he press for rapid sexual involvement early in the relationship?
   b) Does he express a need to dominate sexually, verbally or by behavior? For instance, does he talk about women wanting to be dominated or not meaning it when they say "no"?
   c) Does he make joking or serious statements that suggest irrational jealousy or a feeling that he "owns" you sexually?

Does he have a problem with you having platonic relationships with other men?

d) Does he whine, complain, or pressure you to change your clearly stated sexual boundaries (beyond expressing momentary disappointment or frustration)?

e) Does he refuse to use birth control or consider it your problem? Does he pressure you for unprotected sex?

Extra Credit: Is he currently married or in a committed relationship but pursuing a romantic relationship with you? (Score 5 for this in addition to any other points, no matter how bad his current partner may sound!)

SCORE: _____

11) Gut Feelings

a) Do you find yourself feeling out of control, in over your head, with intense feelings a short time into the relationship?

b) Do you frequently find yourself trying to change your behavior in order to please him? Or find yourself reluctant to speak up when something bothers you?

c) Do you find yourself explaining away any doubts you may have about him?

d) If you let him know you don't like something, does he "explain things" in a way that leaves you more confused? Or say he'll change his behavior and yet continue to do the same things?

e) If he did the same things he's doing with you to your girlfriend, would it bother you?

SCORE: _____

12) Extra Credit: Power Imbalance

Jerks often take advantage of age or position to establish better control over their victims. The following situations are not automatically bad, but are very commonly associated with victimizing behavior on the part of the more powerful person. It is common for older men to look to younger women as partners, because the younger women look up to them and are easier to control. And believe it or not, people sometimes choose professions such as teaching, coaching, or counseling just so they can find potential partners they can control.

You should always be *very* skeptical if someone much older or who has an authority relationship with you wants to date you. And if they are both older AND have a power relationship over you, WATCH OUT – they are probably up to no good!

a) Is the person significantly older than you? (I'd say 5 years if you're 20, 7.5 if you're 30, and 10 years if you're 40.)

Score 1 point if they meet the above criteria. Score 3 if they are more than double the above (i.e., 10 years when you're 20, etc.)

b) Is the person in a relationship where they have power over you?
   1) If they are your teacher, professor, coach, attorney, or other hired professional, score 2.
   2) If they are your doctor, counselor, psychiatrist, clergyman, or other caretaker, score 5.

SCORE: _____

TOTAL SCORE: _____

Here is the scoring:

- 0–10 – Probably fine – relax and enjoy yourself, but check again as needed
- 10–20 – Caution – Jerky signs are emerging – keep screening carefully
- 20–30 – Likely Jerk – set strong boundaries and be prepared to dump him
- 30–40 – Surefire Jerk – get rid of him right away
- 40+ – RUN AWAY – FAST!

There is no way to assure that any relationship will work out the way you want to. But it is possible to detect whether or not someone is genuinely trying to work out a good relationship, or is working to take advantage of you. With some honest self-reflection and the skills outlined in this book, you should be able to tell a good guy from a Jerk with a very high level of accuracy. You may have to let go of some romantic fantasies, but the benefit just may be a genuine relationship with a caring and reliable man that will last long after the romantic honeymoon is over.

Best of fortune to you all, and may the Jerks run the other way when they see you coming!

About the Author

STEVE MCCREA, MS, IS AN EDUCATOR, COUNSELOR AND ADVOCATE who has worked for more than twenty years with survivors of domestic abuse and their children in a variety of settings. He is a 1980 graduate of Oberlin College in Ohio and received his Master's at St. Joseph's University in Philadelphia in 1986. Over the years, he has helped hundreds of women (and a handful of men) escape from and stay away from abusive relationships. He has been the co-chair of the Domestic Violence Intervention Council for Washington County, Oregon, and has participated in the Multnomah County (Oregon) Family Violence Coordinating Council since 2001. He is currently serving on the advisory council of a safe visitation and exchange program for domestic abuse victims in the Portland metropolitan area. Steve has designed and delivered professional trainings on working with domestic abuse victims in the child welfare system and on the impact of domestic abuse on children. He has also volunteered for over nine years as a facilitator for an on-line domestic abuse survivor community, whose members provided the majority of the stories shared in the book.

Steve lives in a classic 1905 house in Portland, Oregon, with Ginny, his wife of over twenty-five years. They have three sons, Patrick, Sean, and Kevin, and a granddaughter, Lucy. He currently works supervising volunteers for the Court Appointed Special Advocates (CASA) program, whose job is to advocate for children in the Oregon foster care system. He spends his free time helping on the survivors' discussion board, writing, bicycling, hiking and watching and filming Kevin's innumerable soccer matches.

RECEIVED
APR 1 8 2013

BY: ....

DATE DUE

GAYLORD			PRINTED IN U.S.A.

CPSIA information can be obtained at www.ICGtesting.com
Printed in the USA
BVOW011126250712

296129BV00006BA/51/P

9 781592 997404